# Street Level Narcotics

## A Patrolman's Guide To Working Street Level Dope

*Daren R. Ellison*

iUniverse, Inc.
New York   Bloomington

Street Level Narcotics
A Patrolman's Guide To Working Street Level Dope

iUniverse books may be ordered through booksellers or by contacting:

iUniverse
1663 Liberty Drive
Bloomington, IN 47403
www.iuniverse.com
1-800-Authors (1-800-288-4677)

ISBN: 978-1-4401-6847-5 (pbk)
ISBN: 978-1-4401-6848-2 (ebk)

Printed in the United States of America

iUniverse rev. date: 9/18/2009

To my wife, Alene. Without your encouragement and support, this book would have never happened. I love you.

To my dad, Danny. You have always been my role model and mentor. If someday I become half the man you are, I will be a fine man.

To my dear friend Tony Carpio. You helped me *truly* find God and develop a clear sense of direction. Without my knowing you, I would have never had the spiritual guidance I needed to complete this book. Thank you.

# contents

Prologue     ix

Chapter One     Intelligence     1

Chapter Two     Making Contacts And Stops     9

Chapter Three     Under-The-Influence     23

Chapter Four     Surveillance     38

Chapter Five     The Arrest And Evidence Collection     47

Chapter Six     The Confidential Informant     57

Chapter Seven     The Controlled Buy     67

Chapter Eight     Language And Psychology     76

Chapter Nine     Documentation     82

Chapter Ten     The Search Warrant     87

Chapter Eleven     The Ruse     96

Chapter Twelve     The Criminal Process     108

Chapter Thirteen     Work Ethics And Integrity     121

Chapter Fourteen     Unorthodox Patrol Procedures     129

Epilogue     137

# prologue

It seems to me law enforcement today has a few areas of expertise that gain recognition from peers and supervisors alike that are often looked upon with awe by new officers. In my experience, those areas were narrowed into narcotics, grand theft autos, and fugitive apprehension. Where I worked, state parole officers and their fugitive apprehension team chased most parolees at large who were notorious and dangerous felons with the aura about them that they would, "Never go back!" Others sat in briefing scribbling license plate numbers to catch an occupied stolen car or, as we called it, a "roller." My area of interest and expertise was in working street-level narcotics and the arrests I made and the experience I gained continue to reward me throughout my career.

This book is written for the young, inexperienced patrol officer who is new to working street-level dope who wants to learn and for the experienced cop who wants to read another's perspective and experience. Although veteran undercover dope and vice cops may find certain chapters useful, this book is written for the uniformed patrol officer who never had the desire or opportunity to join a specialized unit and who is working shifts that leave him oftentimes unsupervised and alone. Regardless of your motivations for reading this book, I am certain you will learn some new tactics and techniques to help you find dope and solve problems in your beat. And, it might help you remember things you have forgotten over the years. This book is broken into simple, easy to read and follow chapters that can be found quickly in the field and can serve as a guide when you are unsure how to proceed in an investigation.

Throughout this book and within the various chapters, I will explain using simple English how and where to find intelligence on drug dealers, users, and locations, how to learn to make citizen contacts, pedestrian stops, and gain confidence with those stops, how to make traffic stops related to narcotics investigations, how to perfect your verbiage and basic psychology in dealing with street-level narcotics offenders, how to determine if a person is under-the-influence of drugs, how and when to make an arrest safely and gather good evidence, how to develop and maintain the confidential informant, how to conduct "road burns," how to conduct surveillance while in a marked patrol car, how to make controlled buys of narcotics, how and when to write and execute search warrants, how to effectively document your arrests to help with convictions and later courtroom testimony, how to improve your work ethics and integrity, and many other things I have learned and used over the years.

I will explain how you can do all of these things, not while working as part of an undercover or plain clothes specialized task force, but as a solo, uniformed, street-level patrolman, working in both rural and metropolitan environments, responding to calls, and conducting basic patrol duties from a marked patrol car. Yes, it can be done and with some unorthodox techniques, perspectives, and "thinking outside the box" it can sometimes be more effective than undercover work and the output of a specialized unit.

When I read something and the author implies he is an expert, I want to know about him and his qualifications. I want to know who he is and why he thinks he has something to teach. By the time you finish reading this book, I am certain you will be able to relate to me, who I am, and when you have read this book, you too will have something to teach. You can be an expert at street-level narcotics by employing some or all of my techniques. If you work patrol, you had better be an expert working street-level dope because everything you do in patrol nowadays is drug-related.

Nearly twelve years ago, I began my career with the Kern County

Sheriff's Office, one of the largest sheriff's departments in California. I have over ten years of experience working in patrol assignments mostly in rural substations and a couple of years in the metropolitan area. I have qualified myself to testify in court as an expert in under-the-influence detection, narcotics possessions, and sales cases. Everything I offer you in this book is based on my own personal, firsthand knowledge. Every idea, wording, question, trick, technique, or experience I discuss, I have seen and done myself. This book is not a compilation of "war stories" or ideas gathered from others or from textbooks I have read. I did not spend six months doing research to get information to write this book. The research began when I hit the street as a solo beat deputy. It comes from me and with the sincere hope it can help you.

I have never been a braggart and those who know me know I have always tried to keep to myself and simply do my job and arrest dopers. Although I now work as a substation detective, I still work directly with patrol and still patrol myself. When time allows, I work street-level dope with my fellow deputies and I help them make basic arrests and improve their skills. My heart has always been and continues to be with the street-level patrol officers who, as I prefer to call them, are the grunts, the backbone, or the infantry of police work. This book is for them.

# Chapter One
# Intelligence

## *LUCK vs. SKILL*

Few things compare in importance when working dope, or any type of investigation for that matter, than intelligence. Without it, you have no idea where to start your hunt and what you should be looking for. Intelligence tells you who you should stop. It helps you turn the pendulum of *Luck vs. Skill* in your favor. It lets you know when and where you should be to get a hook. It saves you time and gives you a much better understanding about what is happening in your beat. For most of my career, I have used intelligence to increase my odds of making arrests and I have been successful. This is what I tell my partners when they ask me how I get so many possession arrests compared to them. I give them this scenario to help them understand how to create their own luck by using intelligence.

*You could train a laboratory monkey to wear a uniform, drive a car, and make a stop. Even a laboratory monkey will eventually get an arrest. Merely being in uniform and making a stop gives you a chance at finding someone to arrest and if you stop everything that moves, you'll probably find someone with a warrant or who is on probation or parole. That's fine and if you search them you might get lucky and find some dope. My estimate is that in a typical low income neighborhood with a moderate amount of crime, you will find dope in about one out of every fifteen or twenty stops if you search for dope.*

*I would call those odds ninety percent luck and ten percent skill. Now, I will be the first to tell you I'll take luck over skill any day. What I actually mean by this is that I prefer to work smarter and create my own luck. How do you create your own luck? You do it by gathering intelligence and making informed rather than random stops. You create your own luck by thinking "outside the box" and using an uncommon approach to a common problem. You make yourself an expert at working street-level dope and you get as much experience as you can from wherever you can. You turn the pendulum of Luck vs. Skill in your favor by gathering intelligence. Below are some accessible means of gathering that intelligence.*

## POLICE REPORTS

Police officers write lots and lots of reports. They are everywhere and unending. Most stations now keep their reports in a computer database and put copies on a spindle. In the substations I worked, the clerks kept the month's reports available and would file them away at the beginning of the month. When I arrived at a new assignment and barely knew my co-workers let alone the criminals, I would sort through the reports dating back about a month or two.

I read the face sheet of every report and I was able to learn a great deal about my partners and the crooks. First, I looked to see which officers were writing "on-sight" or "self-initiated" reports. I wanted to know who was arresting suspects for being under-the-influence and other drug-related charges. I looked to see which of my partners were being aggressive and stopping and arresting people and at what times and locations those arrests occurred. I looked at the booking charges and read the synopsis and began to learn about my partners and which ones I wanted to talk to about the area and ultimately which ones I wanted to work with.

## CO-WORKERS

I could estimate a deputy's experience level by how well his report was written, how much detail was listed, and how he included probable cause and the elements of the crimes. If I saw a pattern where every report a deputy wrote resulted from a call for service, I looked to see if he used the opportunity as a means to make arrests or if he only wrote reports based on the legal requirements or department policy. If I saw no aggressive actions or eagerness to seize opportunities to make an arrest, I categorized that deputy as "average."

Typically, in a substation with ten or twelve deputies assigned, I expected to find three or four followers who didn't mind working and who were willing to follow me around and help. Followers were useful in helping to transport prisoners, fill out paperwork, and assist in searches. There were always one or two "old-timers" who didn't want to do anything, never worked street-level dope, didn't know how to make an under-the-influence arrest, and did as little as possible. I regarded them as generally useless because they couldn't even help me fill out the paper work properly. And even if I caught them on a good day and they did actually try to help, I found myself spending twice as much time correcting their mistakes. I categorized these deputies as useless and a liability. Of the rest, I expected to find one or two who worked street-level dope aggressively and who actually cleaned up an area. Sometimes these deputies were inexperienced and didn't quite understand what they were doing. But, they had the enthusiasm to learn and contribute. This last group I categorized the "go-getters" and those were the ones I found useful.

Those deputies were who I utilized as my springboard to begin to learn the area and the players. I watched those deputies and asked them everything I wanted to know about the area. I asked them where the drug locations were and what kinds of dope they were seeing. I asked about problem locations and parolees at large. If I could get them to tell me and if they knew, I asked which houses they were watching and who was selling dope. Sometimes, it was difficult getting information from them because they considered their information "secret" and they didn't want someone "stealing their thunder." Sometimes they just didn't know. Regardless, I always respected this and if I sensed some resistance, I didn't pry. After all, I already read their reports and I knew who they arrested.

## CITIZEN INFORMANTS

I never worked an assignment where there were no citizen informants. It seems there is always a concerned citizen or "pest" that calls and visits the office frequently wanting to inform us about drug activity. I recall an exceptionally irritating informant who compiled a list of names, addresses, and vehicle license plate numbers he believed were involved in drug activity. Everybody, including me at first, shrugged and walked away from him whenever he approached. If I saw him or people like him walking up to me while I was at a restaurant or taking a coffee break at the local gas station, I would take out my cell phone and start talking like I just got a call. That always worked and if there was an unsuspecting rookie standing nearby, the "pest" honed in on him and not me.

One day, I decided to actually take some time and listen to the guy. When I did, I realized he had tons of useable information deputies didn't. I copied his notes and began using them to make arrest after arrest. Although he was irritating, I learned a valuable lesson about local hermits who seem to have nothing better to do than begin their own investigations. I learned they have more free time to gather information sometimes than I do and I now use them as part of my information pool. Of course, I always verified information they provided. But, when I had no other leads or intelligence, it was a place to start.

## LOCAL COMPUTER DATABASES, CLETS, AND NCIC

When I started my career as deputy, I wasn't too computer literate. I didn't have a personal computer and the Internet was just beginning to blossom. I never took typing in school or worked with computers. I realized, very soon, the importance and value of computers and I made it a point to seek counsel from clerks and others who knew how to access and use our databases. Within a few years, I surpassed most in computer skills and I became the "go to guy" when one was needed.

Regardless of what programs your department uses and what databases you can access, it is imperative to becoming a good dope cop and investigator that you make yourself an expert in using your systems. Although each system operates differently, most contain the same types of information and are connected with other larger databases. When

I was investigating a drug house or the name of a drug user or dealer, there were a few records I checked regularly during my intelligence gathering.

Usually, when I learned the name of someone I hadn't met and didn't otherwise know, I started my information search by checking the local arrest records. I sought a booking photo so I could put a face with the name. Booking photos usually have basic information such as birthdates, driver's license numbers, and addresses. From there, I would check the person's local entries and law enforcement contacts.

Local data would often tell me what types of charges the person had, with whom he associated or had been with during a contact or arrest, where he frequented, and by checking the local database for traffic citations issued, I could learn what type of car he drove. Citations usually included a vehicle description and license plate number and with a license plate number, I could check the registered owner through the Department of Motor Vehicles' database. This gave me another possible name and address to research. Sometimes a doper's car doesn't belong to him. So, by checking the registration, you learn the name of an associate.

When I was trying to find someone who had an extensive criminal history, I would check the local jail records and see who visited him while he was in custody. Most returning criminals didn't have frequent visits during a short stay in jail. If a crook was serving only ten or fifteen days in the county jail and someone came to visit, I figured that person was a close friend or relative and if I couldn't find the suspect, I would find his visitors. Most inmate booking records list a family member to contact in case of an emergency and criminals, regardless of their age or marital status, almost always list their mother. It seems that mothers never move and an address five or six years old often proves current.

After checking local data, I would then broaden my search to include wants and warrant checks in California's statewide criminal database, CLETS. When we checked a person through CLETS, it was connected to NCIC and I could learn if there were any out of state wants or warrants. Within CLETS, I could run the person and learn how many vehicles were registered to him and the year, make, model, and license plate numbers to those cars. Typically, when I learned the name of a possible drug dealer, the information included a partial vehicle description.

Next, I would check and see if the person was on parole or probation. If he was, I would check the court case and see if there were search terms for narcotics, weapons, or stolen property. I would sometimes print a copy of the search terms if I was going to conduct a search pursuant to those terms. I did this to attach to my report later in the event I made an arrest and the probable cause I developed came from my computer investigation.

Computers are only as good as the people using them and their informational value is only limited to your imagination. I developed a routine of areas to check when I was gathering information and you must do the same within your own operating database. Think of all the possible databases you can search and practice using them. Sometimes, you can find other areas within screens you normally look if you explore the system and see what happens if you check here, and then there, and here …

## HUMAN INTELLIGENCE

After I was familiar with a possible dealer or drug house from my computer research, I would often test what I had been told by a citizen informant and what I learned through computer investigations against a drug addict I was questioning during an interview. Since I already knew what I learned, I would ask vague questions to addicts during under-the-influence investigations and try to corroborate the information I gathered. I did this for a couple of reasons.

First, if I could corroborate information I had gathered from my own research, I could determine the truthfulness of the addict by comparing what he told me to the facts I already knew from solid computer evidence. I did this to test his reliability and decide if he could possibly be a useful informant for me. Next, I could use his information about that drug dealer or drug house to corroborate the citizen informant who gave me the information in the first place. This served as a small checks and balances and sometimes later proved useful when I gathered probable cause for a search warrant.

## SURVEILLANCE

The last area of intelligence gathering I used was surveillance. I will discuss how to conduct surveillance on people and houses, while in a marked patrol car, in more detail in a later chapter. But, for the purposes of this section, I include surveillance as part of the information gathering process. When I was able to establish a drug location, I would spend as much time as possible watching the house looking for activity consistent with drug sales. Depending on the volume of calls for service and my beat partner's needs, I would try to allocate forty-five minutes to an hour each night for a week or two and see if there was a steady flow of vehicle and foot traffic coming to and from a particular house or location. During my surveillance, I often learned if there were children at the house, if there were alleys or foot paths leading to and from the house, if there were any noisy barking dogs, what type of lighting conditions surrounded the property, and how visitors came to and went from the house. Sometimes through surveillance, I was able to learn if my target had a spouse or other family members living there. And, I often learned what types of cars the suspect drove and if there were any inoperable lights on the vehicles I could later use as probable cause to make a stop. All of this information sometimes proved very useful when the time came to hit the house for a search or make a stop leaving.

## CREATE YOUR OWN LUCK

You can go to work every day and drive around aimlessly trying to find someone to arrest hoping to find dope. If you stop everything that moves, eventually you'll get lucky and make an arrest. If it's your lucky day, you might even find some dope. If you have the energy and enthusiasm to make thirty stops per shift, go ahead. If you find something, great! We need people like you because the volume of stops you make lets the community know we're there and doing our jobs. If you'd like to make two or three stops and get a good felony possession arrest, then start gathering intelligence and use that information to direct your patrols. Learn who the players are and watch the dope houses. Concentrate on the neighborhoods being plagued with auto burglaries and other property crimes. Make informed stops on cars leaving drug houses. Use intelligence to turn the pendulum of *Luck vs. Skill* in your favor. Follow the techniques I discuss in this book and start teaching yourself how to become an expert at working street-level dope. If you do this, not only will you benefit from the increased self esteem of knowing you are doing a good job and making a difference, but your co-workers and supervisors will know you are working hard. Above all, the community will reap the rewards of your efforts and that alone should be enough to keep you motivated.

Don't be a laboratory monkey running around making mindless stops. Be particular with your stops and try to lower the number of stops per arrest you make in a shift. If you normally make ten to fifteen stops looking for a warrant suspect or something easy, start making informed stops and arrest drivers leaving dope houses for driving under-the-influence. Start searching their cars for dope and see what happens. If you do this sincerely and put forth some effort, I guarantee your percentage of stops to arrests ratio will be closer to five to one. Use intelligence. It is your friend.

# Chapter Two
# Making Contacts
# And Stops

## CONSENSUAL ENCOUNTERS VS. DETENTIONS

I remember going through the academy and hearing the instructors talking about consensual encounters and the legal aspects associated with them. And, when I sat there as a young trainee, I thought they were truly a wonderful thing and I could contact anyone during a consensual. Well, I grew up and after years of stops and citizen contacts and so called "consensual encounters," I learned they were nothing more than "consensual stops." And, I learned that with a little more knowledge of the vehicle code and case law, I didn't need to do anything consensually. I learned I could stop and detain nearly everyone legally.

The problem I saw with consensual encounters is that they were virtually never, truly consensual. I learned defense attorneys know how to effectively turn a consent search into an unlawful detention by describing to a judge during a suppression motion how, "My client wasn't free to leave." Here's the picture painted:

*A guy is walking down the sidewalk at night time alone doing nothing wrong and minding his own business. A police officer pulls along side him abruptly and shines a million candle power spotlight on him. He keeps walking not looking at the spotlight. The officer rolls down his window and yells to him, "Hey!" So he stops, thinking he is being detained, and the cop asks, "How's it going tonight? Can I talk to you for a minute?" He knows the cop is going to get pissed off and arrest him if he doesn't stop, so he does. The officer makes contact, learns he is high, arrests him for being under-the-influence, searches him, and finds dope. Good luck with that one in court.*

Now, take that same scenario and turn it into a detention. Articulate the time of night, "It was two o'clock in the morning." Describe the suspect's clothing, "It was summertime, 80 degrees outside, and the person was wearing a coat." Describe the suspect's demeanor, "I shined my spotlight on him and he turned his head away from me and put his hands inside his pockets." List how many drug arrests you have made in that neighborhood during those hours etc. Give more information to paint the picture you want the judge or jury to see. Here's an example of a typical police report documenting a consensual encounter:

*I was on routine patrol driving in a marked sheriff's patrol car. I saw JONES walking on the sidewalk. For officer safety reasons, I shined my spotlight on him and he kept walking away from me. I yelled to him, "Hey!" And JONES stopped. I walked up to him and I asked, "Can I talk to you for a minute?"*

Articulate a little more, add more detail, and turn this same scenario into a detention:

*I was on routine patrol driving in a marked sheriff's patrol car. I saw JONES walking on the sidewalk. I wished to speak with him and for officer safety reasons I shined my spotlight on him. When I did, he looked back at me and appeared nervous. I watched him reach inside his right front pant's pocket and toss something into the bushes next to where he walked. He looked back at me again two or three times and tried to avoid looking at my car. His pace increased and I saw his steps grow longer. He walked behind a parked car out of my spotlight and stopped. I believed he was waiting for me to drive passed him. It was nearly midnight and about ten minutes before I saw him, I heard an alarm coming from a vehicle in the area. JONES was wearing dark colored clothing and wore a dark colored backpack and gloves. It was nearly 70 degrees outside and it was not cold. I found his behavior suspicious because in the past two weeks I made four drug-related arrests within two blocks of this area. In the past month, there have been at least four reported auto burglaries and two residential burglaries within two miles of where I saw JONES walking. I stopped JONES to investigate him for possible criminal activity.*

Which of these two scenarios do you think would look better in court? I understand the second may be stretching a little and not all scenarios apply here, but I did that purposefully to get you thinking about other circumstances that could turn a consensual encounter into a good, lawful detention. All you have to do is watch a little more closely, be a little more familiar with your beat and the surroundings, and articulate with a little more detail in your report and you can have a good, lawful, detention instead of a potentially weak consensual encounter.

## PEDESTRIAN STOPS

When you have done your research and gathered intelligence about a possible drug location, the easiest stops to make and those with the highest potential for a felony drug arrest are pedestrian stops. If you watch a person walk up to a drug dealer's house, go inside, and leave in about five minutes or so, you have a very good chance of turning a pedestrian stop into a felony drug possession arrest. Think about it. If that person just purchased dope and he is walking, where can he possibly hide it to avoid being arrested?

Years ago, a co-worker of mine who I worked with regularly and admired, who was also experienced in making dope arrests, told me about pedestrian stops that if you see a person walking he saw you about five or ten steps before you saw him. He elaborated and said therefore, once you make a person stop and are looking for drugs, backtrack about fifteen or twenty feet and you'll be surprised how many times the person tossed a crank pipe or dope in the gutter or bushes just before the stop. This made sense to me and after he said this I started searching the ground and area around my person stops and was a little more thorough. Sure enough, I started to find some more dope and made a few more drug possession arrests.

The most common probable cause I use for making pedestrian stops is the vehicle code violation for a pedestrian walking in the roadway.

If I can't find a legal violation for the stop when I watch someone leave a dope house, then I articulate my knowledge and experience about the house they just left and I stop them to investigate possible drug activity. But if I can, I make a "wall stop" (discussed later) and develop independent probable cause for the stop. If you watch people walk long enough, they are going to leave the sidewalk and walk in the middle of the road. Usually, they do this to avoid charging pit bulls trying to get through a fence to eat them. Regardless of the reason, in California, and likely in most states, walking in the roadway is an infraction and a lawful reason for a detention. Sometimes, I watch them jaywalk and I stop them for this reason. Jaywalking, however, doesn't usually apply in residential neighborhoods.

Once I know I have a lawful reason to make a stop, I get as close as possible before they hear me and then I shine my spotlight on them. Mostly, this pertains to nighttime stops. But, minus the spotlight, I do the same thing during the daytime. Of course you can still use your spotlight during daytime. Then, I close the distance between them and me as quickly as possible. This serves a couple of purposes. One, it gives them less chance to run or retrieve a weapon. Second, if they have a weapon or dope on them, it gives them less time to react and try to hide the drugs or weapon before I catch up to them. To some, accelerating toward a pedestrian seems excessive, but in my experience, it works. I have watched other officers slow play pedestrian stops and I have seen many foot pursuits where the suspect got away. And, I have been there and heard neighbors or passers-by tell us later the person tossed something before the stop.

One evening I was working in the metro patrol area and responded to the call of possible drug activity. The caller told us there was a white male wearing a "wife beater" t-shirt riding a bicycle and selling drugs. We arrived just a couple of minutes after the call came out and we drove around the area looking for the would-be drug dealer. My partner found the guy riding his bicycle down the alley. My partner put his spotlight on him and then stopped him a short distance later. We checked the guy and found no dope on him. He was on probation and subject to search for drugs. We checked him and he wasn't high so we completed a field interview card on him and let him go. We sat there talking for a few minutes after the guy left and an old man from the yard where we stopped the bicyclist walked up to us. He said, "You guys missed something." And he pointed to a plastic sandwich bag on the ground inside his yard. The old man said he saw the bicyclist throw the bag into his yard just before we stopped him. Sure enough, he tossed a bag of dope.

Finding dope or weapons after you have stopped people and then released them, is both embarrassing and time consuming. You end up writing a report with nobody in custody. To the public, you look completely incompetent and you feel like a fool. My motto when working street-level dope has always been, "*If I have to write a report, someone better be in jail.*" It is going to happen sometime in your career. I promise. But, make sure the times you write possession reports after you have released your suspect are far and few between.

## BICYCLE STOPS

Next to pedestrian stops, bicycle stops are the easiest to make and find dope. As with a person walking, a person on a bicycle has few areas he can hide dope or weapons. Bicyclists, however, are more likely than a person on foot to violate the vehicle code. Nearly everyone riding a bicycle rides on the wrong side of the road and doesn't stop at stop signs. Bicyclists also tend to ride on the sidewalk. During darkness, only bicyclists who have been stopped on a bike at night before have a headlamp and rear light. Most are riding without lights in the dark. All of these violations give you a lawful reason to stop a person riding a bicycle.

After I make a bicycle stop, I leave the person on his bike. Some officers prefer to have him step off his bike. It is a personal choice. I always choose to keep him on the bike because I find him less threatening straddling the bar and seat than when he is off the bike standing. I conduct my entire investigation with him still seated or straddling the seat. Usually, the suspect holds on to the handle bars and this gives me a good view of his hands and body movements. If he decides to fight or run, he has to make overt movements to either get off the bike or try to ride away. I have never had a person on a bike run away from me after I stopped him.

Like pedestrians, bicyclists probably saw you long before you saw them. Therefore, be sure to search the area where you stopped the person on the bike. By virtue of the speed bicycles travel as compared to pedestrians, it is more difficult to find items discarded before the stop. A bicyclist could have seen you a block before you saw him and your search for drugs or weapons may extend an entire block. If I saw the person leaving a drug house and I was certain he just purchased drugs, I would take the time to search the sidewalk and yards to the nearest corner. It is more difficult to pin the contraband you find on him the further away it is from the stop, but it can still be done. Sometimes, after I stopped a bicyclist and I arrested him for being under-the-influence and I had him detained in my car, I would back track looking for drugs. When I found dope, I would return to the car with it and show it to him as if I expected to have found something. Then, I would read him his Miranda Advisal and ask him about the dope. When he denied it belonging to him, I would tell him, as a matter of fact, I saw him throw it down. I would ask him a question like, *"Come on man. Do you really think I would stop you for not having a light? Of course not. Dude, I saw you toss this down."*

If a ruse doesn't work, you have a weak case unless you did in fact see him toss something down near where you found dope. If he doesn't admit to throwing the item you seized, walk back to where you found it and start looking for evidence. Talk to any neighbors standing outside and try to develop a witness. If that doesn't work, look for bicycle tracks next to where you found the dope. If there are tracks, take a photograph of them and try to compare them with the suspect's bike tracks. Sometimes, you can find enough circumstantial evidence to establish the person tossed the dope before the stop, even though you did not see him toss it. If you just can't prove it and he is high, arrest him for being under-the-influence and book the dope anyway. While wearing latex gloves to prevent contamination, try and lift a latent fingerprint off the packaging used to seal the dope and hope for a fingerprint match with your suspect's prints through AFIS (Automated Fingerprint Identification System.) If you lift a print, which is doubtful because it is difficult to lift a useable print off a wrapped piece of plastic, and that print is actually matched to your suspect, submit it to the district attorney to have additional charges filed. Waiting to file possession charges until you have proven it belonged to your suspect shows the attorneys your thoroughness and understanding of reasonable doubt, which is the highest standard of proof in the American criminal justice system.

# TRAFFIC STOPS

Next to residential or building searches, traffic stops and vehicle searches are good places to find larger quantities of drugs. Drugs have to be transported and vehicles offer the dealer the best protection against discovery. Of course, in major narcotics investigations, boats and planes can be used. But, in street-level dope vehicles are the main means of transportation. Dealers use their own personal cars to make small and frequent deliveries around town and the chances of finding a dealer driving in possession of drugs are very good when you have developed your intelligence.

One good thing about making a vehicle stop leaving a dealer's house is you can follow the car and make the stop several blocks or miles away. There's nothing worse than stopping a person, bicyclist, or car down the street from the dope house. Even if the dealer doesn't know you made the stop immediately, someone passing by is likely to tell him. You can easily dry up a good fishing hole if you do that. Unless circumstances dictate otherwise, pick your stops as far away from your target house as possible.

When making a car stop, use vehicle code violations as your reasoning for making the stop. Watch the car arrive at the house, wait for it to leave, and develop independent probable cause to stop it for some vehicle code violation. My personal preference is to try and stop the car for equipment violations as opposed to violating the rules of the road. My reasoning is that an equipment violation i.e. an inoperable license plate lamp, can be photographed and used as evidence later in court. A moving violation, such as failing to come to a complete stop at a stop sign, is debatable. The crook is going to say he stopped and all you have is your word that he did not. You can't photograph a moving violation without a dash mounted video recorder. Once you have made the stop, there are some proven techniques to use during the initial contact and investigation that will help you tilt the pendulum of *Luck vs. Skill* in your favor. These techniques will help you create your own luck in finding dope on traffic stops.

# TRAFFIC STOP TECHNIQUES

To begin to learn and develop confidence in yourself and your abilities, try to stop cars with only the driver and at most, one passenger.

Remember, most of the time you are working alone or with only one partner. It is more difficult to conduct an effective drug search with three occupants in the car. It can be done and many experienced officers do it regularly. But for now, try to deal with only one or two people at a time. It's safer, more likely to produce the desired results, and it's easier.

## FEMALES

If you are a male officer and have no female officer working with you, try to avoid stopping cars with female passengers. If the female is the driver and sole occupant, you might get lucky and find dope in her purse or in her pockets. But, if you stop a car leaving a dope house with a female passenger and a male driver, your odds of getting dope are greatly reduced. Remember, you want to use more skill than luck. Most smart drug dealers and users are going to hide their dope either on or in the female passenger and your ability to find it is really hindered. Without a search warrant, you are not going to find the "forty sac" she shoved inside her as you were making the stop. Even if you arrest her for being under-the-influence and take her to jail, jail staff are not going to strip search her if she is going to be cited and released on a misdemeanor.

Here are a couple of tricks you can use with a female suspect you think is holding dope. Tell her a canine officer is on the way with his drug sniffing dog and he is going to smell to see if she has drugs on her. Tell her the dog usually bites the area where the drugs are hidden and if she has drugs in her, the dog is going to bite her. Now, we all know canine officers can't legally allow their dogs to sniff and bite narcotics on people. But, crooks don't know that. Sometimes, the female will admit she has dope in her and she can retrieve it for you. Be sure to wear gloves before she pulls it out and hands it to you! Another trick is to tell her she is going to jail and will be strip searched. If she has drugs on her and brings those drugs into the jail, it is an additional felony charge. But, if she gives you the drugs now on the street, it is a lesser charge and she will be released sooner with lesser bail. Sometimes, that works. Be creative and find a ruse that works for you. If nothing works and you believe a female is holding dope and she is under-the-influence, take her to jail for the lesser misdemeanor. You'll gain respect from the crooks as not being stupid if you arrest them for lesser charges when you know they are guilty of more severe charges but just can't prove it.

# FORCING THE CONTACT AT THE CAR

Probably the biggest mistake I made as a young deputy and a reoccurring mistake I see many officers make now when working street-level dope is returning to their patrol car during the stop. I know how dangerous traffics stops can be and I have seen all those videos of traffic stops turned bad. It is normal for us to want to return to the safety of our cars during a traffic stop. Typically, we stop the car, make contact with the driver, grab his driver's license, and then retreat to the safety of our car. We use our car as a barrier between us and the suspect and feel comfortable that if he comes out shooting we have a bunch of steel and metal to hide behind. I understand this and I too feel safe standing behind my trunk waiting for dispatch to return with a driver's license and warrant check. But, when working street-level dope, you must stay with the people in the car after the stop and continue to "force the contact."

In the academy, we learned the most dangerous time for us during the traffic stop is the approach to the car. Right? Well, I agree. So, once we have walked up to the car, either on the driver's side or the passenger side, and we have survived that fatal approach once, why would we want to return to our car just to check someone's license status and see if they are on probation or parole? Because once we find out, we have to approach their car again. This is where you have to "force the contact" and stay with the driver and other occupants of the car.

Today, we all have hand held radios and most of the time we can conduct our business with our portable radios. So, when I am making a dope stop, I stay with the vehicle and ask my series of questions, standing right there next to the car, keeping everyone in view. If there are passengers seated in the back, I tell them to put their hands on the seat in front of them so I can watch their hands. Then, I conduct my traffic stop business with them in clear view. Sometimes, especially on busy roads and freeways, I approach on the passenger side. If the driver is alone, I make him reach across the passenger seat and through the passenger window. This keeps him stretched out and less of a threat. Then, I begin my series of routine questions to try and find a reason to arrest him.

Years ago, my department introduced a format we were supposed to use when making contacts during traffic stops. And, if I stopped a family leaving church service, I used that format. It was polite and considerate and was designed to place the person stopped at ease. But when working street-level dope and making dope stops and dealing with thugs, I throw that out the window. I try to keep dopers comfortable and off their guard. I want them to think I just stopped them for a minor traffic violation. But, I do it somewhat differently than the nice cop format. During a dope stop, my whole intention is to get the person into handcuffs as quickly as possible and search him for dope. The faster you can do this, the better your chances are of finding the dope he just purchased. The fastest way to get the driver into handcuffs during a traffic stop is to arrest him for being an unlicensed driver.

When I first start my contact during a dope traffic stop, I tell the driver why I stopped him and I ask to see his driver's license. If he doesn't have a driver's license, I ask him, "Why not?" If he tells me it's suspended or he never had one issued, he is under arrest. I have him open his door, while still seated, turn toward the passenger side of the car and place his hands behind his back. If I can, I handcuff the driver while he is still seated. In my opinion, during on-sight or self initiated drug enforcement stops, it is safer to arrest someone seated in a car than having him stand up and outside the car. My argument is that he is less likely to assault me while seated than standing outside the car. Then, once the cuffs are on, I have him stand up. If there is a passenger, I keep the driver at his door and search him in front of the passenger. I keep facing the passenger during the entire search. My whole intention is to not leave anyone in the vehicle alone without being able to watch them. I try to limit the opportunities a person has to hide dope. If the driver is alone, I walk him back to my car.

There, I search him for weapons first and then I dive into his pockets looking for drugs. The most common place I find drugs on people is in their coin pocket. If I don't find it there, I search all the pockets. If I still haven't found dope, I look in their cigarette pack and their wallet. No luck? I search their socks. If I still haven't found their dope, I have them take off their shoes. If it's not in their shoes and I am certain I searched them thoroughly, I make sure my back seat is clear and then I sit them in my car. If I am working alone, I lock them in my car and go search theirs. Sometimes, they will retrieve the dope from wherever they had it hidden and they will dump it in my car. That's fine because

I always search my back seat before I put someone there. So, if I find dope in my car, I know who dumped it.

## VEHICLE SEARCH

When I am searching a car I saw leaving a dope house, I look in the obvious places first. If I was watching a drug house and I saw a car arrive, the driver exit and go into the house, return a few minutes later and go directly to the driver's seat and drive away, I am going to focus my search in the driver's area. Makes sense right? Why waste time initially searching for some secret squirrel hidden compartment I have seen only twice in my career when I saw the driver go directly back to the car? This is where surveillance intelligence helps you save time and effort.

Dope is like a candy bar. If you went into a store and bought a candy bar, would you hide it someplace so difficult to find it would take you hours and fifty different tools to eat? No. And neither would dopers. Always search the obvious places first. If you "forced contact" during the traffic stop, they had no time to hide their dope in the vents or under the dash. It will probably be wedged between the seat cushions, under the seat, tossed in the back, in the center console, or on the ground outside the driver's door. Take notice if the windows were already rolled down at the time of the stop. If so, look on the ground around the car.

Years ago, I developed a citizen informant whose husband was a doper. I had arrested him five times for drug charges and she later told me her husband used to hide his dope in the rearview mirror. She told me he broke the plastic tab from behind the lever you flip to divert rear headlights shining in the mirror. Then, the mirror was hollow and he could store his dope inside it and flip the tab down. The unsuspecting officer was unlikely to find the dope and he used this spot during two of the arrests I made. I never found his dope until she told me about the hiding spot. A couple of weeks after I learned this, I stopped him leaving a drug dealer's house. I arrested him again for being under-the-influence and I searched his truck. This time, I found his dope in the rearview mirror. I have checked the mirror in every car I have searched since and I have found dope there three other times.

There are unlimited areas a person can use to hide dope. Your training and experience will help you find it and the more you find the more experience you gain. The more experience you have, the less you will have to work to find dope during your searches. If you are certain there is dope in a car and you just can't seem to find it, call for another officer if one is available and have him search behind you. Sometimes, a fresh pair of eyes and a different perspective will solve the puzzle. If you plan on using a canine to conduct your search, don't contaminate the car by searching it yourself first. Let the dog go through the car and then search it yourself. Just because a dog doesn't find dope doesn't mean it's not there.

## OTHER WAYS TO GET INTO THE CAR

If after you contact the driver he has a valid driver's license and he hands it to you, make certain it is in fact a driver's license and not just an identification card. Many times, dopers will hand you an identification card passing it off as a driver's license. If they do have a valid driver's license, ask them, "When was the last time you were arrested?" I know, I know. It sounds so harsh automatically assuming someone has been arrested. But when dealing with dopers, they are all high, they all have dope on them, they are all on probation, they all have warrants, they are all unlicensed driver's, and they are all parolees, unless they prove to you otherwise.

If the driver tells you he was arrested six months ago, ask him, "For what?" Remember, you are digging for facts to use to establish a reason to search for dope. If he says he was arrested for possession, ask him, "Of dope or stolen property?" Narrow your field of questions. If he admits to being arrested for drug-related charges, ask him, "So, are you on probation subject to search?" If he tells you he is on probation and he believes he has search terms for narcotics, take his word and conduct a probation search. Have him step out of the car and search him for drugs. Then do just like I described before. Seat him in your car. Before you start your search of his car, confirm his probation status first.

If the driver is not on probation or parole and has a valid driver's license, ask him when he last used. You don't need to specify "what" he used because you are speaking his language. (I will discuss verbiage and colloquial language later) He will understand what you mean. If he tells you he hasn't used for three days, this usually translates into three hours. Regardless of his answer, start to perform a drug evaluation. While he is still sitting in the driver's seat, determine if he is under-the-influence of a controlled substance. If he is and you can't find any other reason to search him and the car for dope, arrest him for being high and follow the above technique I described for getting him out of the car and into yours.

## CONSENSUAL VEHICLE SEARCH

I have never conducted a consensual vehicle search and found dope. In my opinion, there is nothing weaker in court than a consent search of a vehicle. If you can't establish probable cause to arrest someone and conduct a lawful search of his car incident to that arrest, the chances of you getting permission to search, searching, and actually finding dope are so slim you are better off cutting your losses and stopping another car leaving a different dope house. I hardly consider consent as part of my repertoire and I use it seldom and only as a last resort. The reality is that when working street-level dope you should be able to find probable cause to make an arrest and you don't need consent. Maybe narcotics officers working a major drug trafficking operation might use consent when some wealthy, non- user, businessman is tipped off by an informant as having a large quantity of dope in some hidden compartment in his Mercedes. But in my opinion as a uniformed patrol officer, consent is weak and can easily be beaten in court. Rely on probable cause. It is your friend.

## WALL STOPS

I remember working out of the metro patrol division one afternoon and was told to telephone a sergeant in narcotics. I called him and he told me his unit received information from an informant a person was driving a white Camaro and was in possession of a large quantity of methamphetamine. He told me who was driving the car, where the car was driving to, and when. The sergeant told me he needed a uniformed officer to make a "wall stop" on the Camaro and find a reason to search the car for the drugs. I told him, "Sure sarge. No problem." And then I asked, "What's a wall stop?"

A "wall stop" is a stop made on a vehicle or person independent from information known beforehand. So, instead of stopping a car because an informant told you there was a large quantity of methamphetamine inside, you are stopping it for an unrelated traffic violation and need to develop independent probable cause to search the car for the drugs. You are creating an imaginary wall between the information you had before the stop and the probable cause developed after the stop.

So in essence, every time you stop a person, bicyclist, or a car, leaving a dealer's house, you are making a "wall stop" when you stop them for a violation and develop independent probable cause to search them for drugs. When you do find drugs and make an arrest, your report starts where you saw the person violate the vehicle code section. It doesn't start where you were watching a drug house and saw the person walking away from there. The benefit is that you protect your knowledge, and later informants, that a particular person or house is selling drugs and you can make several arrests before going after the dealer himself. When I do make arrests leaving a particular house and I don't have status on the house, meaning there is nobody there on probation or parole and I will need a search warrant to search the house later, I keep copies of those reports to use as reference. This information is crucial when writing the probable cause declaration on a search warrant affidavit for a search warrant of the house and drug dealer. (I will discuss search warrants in a later chapter)

## PRACTICE AND VOLUME

Throughout this book, I reiterate the importance of making volumes of stops and practicing your skills. It is paramount that you make hundreds of person and vehicle stops to gain confidence and experience when working street-level dope. You can't read about how to determine if someone is high and become a drug recognition expert. There are too many variables and possible scenarios. If you are being a slug and you just wait for someone to call dispatch and tell them, "I'm high" begging, "Please come and arrest me," you aren't going to develop the necessary skills to be effective. You must get as much practice and volume as possible dealing with dopers to become a good street-level dope cop. You owe it to yourself, your beat partners, your department, and the community to become an expert at working street-level dope. Your department hired you and I have given you the tools in this book. The rest is up to you.

# Chapter Three
## Under-The-Influence

### EPIDEMIC

In the early 1980s, we began to acknowledge there was a drug problem in the United States. President Ronald Reagan declared war on drugs, "Just say no" became a commonplace slogan, DEA agents were being captured working under cover in foreign countries, and in 1983 Los Angeles Police Chief Darryl Gates introduced the D.A.R.E program into elementary schools. Drugs were everywhere and causing worldwide problems. Well folks, the war isn't over and we didn't win.

I estimate ninety percent of everything we do in law enforcement is drug-related. If we take a residential burglary report, somehow it is drug-related. The suspects probably sold the items for dope. If we are sent to a domestic disturbance, chances are someone is under-the-influence of an illegal street drug or alcohol. If we respond to the victim of a stabbing, nine times out of ten the person was stabbed over a drug-related issue or the suspect was under-the-influence of drugs. When we are asked to assist Child Protective Services to check the welfare of children, it is almost always drug-related.

If a twenty year old man is receiving disability and can't work, it's because he was injured at the job he had for three months. Why? Because he smokes crank and his body is robbed of its calcium needed to keep his bones strong and his potassium levels are so low his muscles and ligaments are easily torn and damaged. It is drug-related. And when that man doesn't work and needs a drug fix, he steals. And then, since he doesn't have a job and all he does is smoke dope all day he gets horny watching porn and he knocks up a tweaker chick and she squeezes out four kids and waddles into the welfare office. And, he is locked up half of the time on drug-related charges. And she hocks her food stamps to buy dope and the kids run around unattended in the front yard starved, dirty, and barefoot and the U.S. Postal lady sees this and calls the cops and they call the social worker and the kids are taken into protective custody and mom goes to jail. Then, the kids grow up in foster homes and the foster dad rapes the six year old boys and they grow up to be teenage pedophiles who use drugs and the cycle continues and the next generation of drug addicts is born and on and on and on ...

Everything we do is drug-related. If you don't believe this, then quit your job and become a long haul truck driver or a librarian. Save the rest of the world from your ignorance and don't be a cop. If you're realistic, you know all we do is drug-related. Develop a plan to be part of the solution. The best thing you can do to be part of the solution and not part of the problem is to make yourself a drug recognition expert and arrest every doper you can.

## MAKE YOURSELF AN EXPERT

Before you can become a good street-level dope cop, you have to become an expert at the under-the-influence arrest. If you are new to patrol, before you seriously try to start making drug possession arrests and taking down drug dealers and working confidential informants, become a drug recognition expert. Make at least one hundred under-the-influence arrests and become so proficient at determining if someone used drugs, what types of drugs he used, and how long ago, that you can pull up to an intersection, look over at the guy in the car next to you, and know if he is high or not. If your department has available drug recognition training, do everything you can to attend those training classes. Don't expect your boss to be a nice guy and send you. Earn the right to go to training. You earn that right through your job performance. If you are making one or two under-the-influence arrests each shift, your boss is going to know you are motivated and you work. When schools become available and he can only send one or two employees, he is going to send the ones who deserve to go.

If your boss doesn't take the initiative to find training opportunities, find the schools yourself. Tell your boss about upcoming training you found and let him know you'd like to attend. If he doesn't send you, pay for the training and send yourself. I have paid for my own training and gone on my days off. Remember, POST training is reimbursable. Your department knows this. Use this as a way of convincing your department to send you to training if money becomes the issue.

Aside from what you learn from your drug arrests, research drugs and their effects. The Internet has chat rooms for addicts to discuss how they use drugs. There are chat rooms for users, dealers, and drug cooks. Log into them and start talking. You won't believe the information addicts have. Everything you learn goes toward your knowledge and expertise. Once you begin to make more and more under-the-influence arrests, the district attorney will probably have you qualify on the stand as an expert. When I started testifying in my own drug cases as an expert, I began to get subpoenas as an expert witness for other officer's cases. This can be a pain because you get inundated with subpoenas and start to spend your life in court, but it is part of the process. You establish a reputation with judges and attorneys just like you do with criminals.

## SYMPTOMOLOGY VARIABLES

Drug recognition is not an exact science. It is more of an art. There are so many variables to consider during an under-the-influence evaluation that even the best recognition expert can only make an educated guess. That's okay. The reason why it is so inexact is because street-level drugs are uncontrolled. If you have a tooth pulled and the dentist prescribes you a certain milligram painkiller, the effects of that painkiller can be accurately predicted because it is consistent and has been tested in a laboratory before being used. Methamphetamine concocted in some tweaker's garage at one o'clock in the morning is uncontrolled and its effects are unpredictable.

If an eighteen-year-old 120 pound female snorts a line of crank for the first time, her symptoms will likely be very different and more exaggerated than a forty-year-old 200 pound man who has used daily since he was twenty. This is the same for any drug. A long time heroin user will react differently than a new user. Sex, size, age, race, and other factors determine the symptoms you are going to see and use in your drug evaluation and arrest. If someone smokes very good quality marijuana with a high concentration of THC, you might see symptoms similar to methamphetamine use. Many times, you are seeing both. Drug addicts are poly users and it isn't uncommon to find a tweaker who has smoked some crank, a joint, who is taking Vicodin, and drinking alcohol.

I will give you the basic signs and symptoms I use to try and determine what drugs a person has recently used. Some of the tests I use are part of the standard DAR (Drug Abuse Recognition) seven steps process for determining drug usage and others are not. Remember, you must follow your department's guidelines when making under-the-influence arrests. Every agency has its own format and many use different definitions. It is your responsibility to know how to complete your forms and meet your department's requirements. Below, I have listed the major symptoms I look for and use to develop my probable cause to arrest someone when I believe they are under-the-influence of certain drugs. There are countless other drugs, but I am only listing the ones I have seen from the arrests I have made. Don't forget, sometimes the best way to know what drug a person has used is to ask him and let him tell you.

## METHAMPHETAMINE SYMPTOMS

Methamphetamine is the undisputed leader when it comes to the most prominent drug abused in my county. Ninety-nine percent of the time when I am talking about a drug addict or experience, meth is the drug I am talking about. I have seen some ecstasy, PCP, tar heroin, cocaine, peyote, and prescription pills like Oxycontin. But most of my drug arrests were crank related.

## FINGER TREMORS AND OBVIOUS SIGNS

One of the first things I look for when I stop dopers is their body movements. When people are high on meth, sometimes they have jerky body movements. Their fingers will twitch and they can't stand still.

Those are very obvious signs. I look at their general appearance. I look to see if their hair is dirty and stringy. I look at their complexion and see if they have sores and pimples on their face. The toxicity levels in their bodies are often so high with chemicals, their skin becomes unhealthy and their diets are sometimes so horrible, they break out with pimples, rashes, and sores.

Drugs rob the body of calcium. This causes the protective enamel on the teeth to disappear and when it does, the teeth start to rot and decay. Long time meth users often have horribly rotten teeth. So, I look for this. I smell their breath. I don't like to, but sometimes when you're talking to tweakers, you can't help but smell their rancid breath. This is caused from bad oral hygiene and the body's reaction and attempts to expel the toxins. Most of these symptoms result from the body's attempt to heal itself.

After I have looked for these overt signs and symptoms, which I can do while standing there talking, I start to look for more obscure signs of recent drug use. At night, I hold my flashlight on the person and I look at his pupils. If it is dark and I have shined my Streamlight into his face and his pupils are obviously large and dilated, I start to look more closely.

## THE EYES AND EYELIDS

The first thing I usually do during a drug evaluation is ask the person when he last used. This is always a good place to start. If he admits to using great! But if he doesn't, keep looking. Ask him to close his eyes. Tweakers sometimes have eyelid tremors. I have seen eyelid tremors so bad it literally looked like the person was blinking his eyes as fast as he could. I could see the whites of his eyes and his pupils as his eyelids were fluttering. These symptoms are extreme, but most are slight. They may be quick little tremors and you usually have to shine your light on the closed eyelids to see them. If you see tremors, hold your light just off to the side of his closed eyelid and ask him to open his eyes. When he opens his eyes, your light should show his pupils and you can see if the pupils constrict. If he's sober, they should. If they stay dilated, you are in business. If you don't have a penlight available, you can check his pupils with your main flashlight by holding the light by the lens and diffusing the brightness by covering the light partially with you hand.

## PULSE RATE

If I believe a person is under-the-influence after a preliminary check of his eyes, I ask to check his pulse. Most people are nervous when they are stopped by the cops. I understand this and I take a slightly elevated pulse rate into account. Most normal people who are standing still or who have just been walking casually will have a pulse rate of between 60 to 90 beats per minute. A sober person who was walking might have a pulse rate of 90 beats per minutes. When he is stopped by the police, I would expect his pulse rate to be about 100 to 105 for the first few minutes. If he was doing nothing wrong, I would expect his pulse rate to drop below 100 and closer to 90 or less. Don't put too much consideration on your first pulse rate if you stop a bicyclist or a person running. Spend about ten to fifteen minutes with him and check his pulse again later. If a bicyclists' pulse rate is 130 after he has been sitting on his bike for ten minutes during a detention, you're in business. Don't believe him when he tells you his pulse is high because he is just nervous. He's high.

When I check someone's pulse, I almost always take it on their right wrist and in the same place. When I use the same place, I can find it easily and quickly. Because I am touching people's skin and they are usually nasty, I limit my contact to fifteen seconds. I take their pulse and multiply it by four. This pulse rate isn't going to be as accurate as one counted for an entire minute. But, within a few beats per minute, it is accurate enough for a drug evaluation. Remember, it is an art and not an exact science.

Depending on how much meth a person used and how long ago he used, I would expect a person under-the-influence to have a pulse rate between 110 and 140 beats per minute. If a person is coming down and he is on the last couple of hours of a drug high, his pulse might be about 105 to 110 beats per minute. If he used within minutes of you stopping him, his pulse could be 160 to 180 beats per minute or more. If you are having a hard time counting his pulse because it's so fast, he's high.

# RHOMBERG STAND

This field examination is now nearly universal and I don't know an agency or officer who doesn't use this as a means to determine suspected drug use. Unlike most of the drug influence evaluations, the Rhomberg Stand or Challenge is medically proven to be accurate. It is a means to determine a person's internal clock and it is a time estimation challenge. When I perform this challenge, I follow this format.

I have the person stand facing me with his arms down by his sides and his feet together. I tell him to tilt his head back and close his eyes. I tell him that when I say "begin," he is to estimate thirty seconds in his mind and not count out loud. I tell him to open his eyes and say "now" or "okay" when he thinks thirty seconds has passed. I look at my watch and when the second hand is on an easy number to count from, I tell him to begin. I observe him and look at my watch periodically. When he tells me to "stop," I look to see how many seconds have passed. I've had a lot of dopers ask me, "How'd I do?" And, I tell them.

During the challenge, I look for certain signs and symptoms while he is counting in his mind. I look at his Adam's apple and see if it is thumping. Sometimes, you can see the pulse in the carotid artery when he tilts his head back. To me, the Adam's apple bumping is an indicator of recent drug use. I also look for muscle rigidity. If his muscles are tight and they are unusually stiff, that is a sign of a stimulant. I check to see if he has eyelid tremors and I watch his hands. I have never received a negative urine test when I saw a person's finger's flicking and twitching uncontrollably during a Rhomberg test. Never. If you see those things, you've got a good hook.

A normal sober person will estimate thirty seconds in 25-35 seconds. The courts allow for a plus or minus ten count margin for error (20-40.) I have performed the Rhomberg test on myself and my friends many times and we were always able to estimate within a few seconds. If you explain the test to a doper, he tilts his head back, you say "begin" and fifteen seconds later he tells you to "stop," you've got a very important piece of probable cause needed to make a good under-the-influence arrest. If you tell the person to "begin" and three seconds later he tells you to "stop," ask him if he believed thirty seconds have just passed. If he does, he's high.

Some drug influence evaluation worksheets have a diagram of a person facing forward and to the side. That is listed so you can mark in inches the amount the body swayed side to side and front to back during the challenge. If you think someone is high on speed only, he shouldn't move much. If he's drunk, expect a lot of movement. If he's on heroin, he might fall asleep during the challenge and fall over. Be aware of this and be prepared to react. Naturally, a central nervous system depressant like alcohol and opiates will cause a person's time estimation to be very slow. I have seen a person count to two minutes and believe thirty seconds had passed. The more drug arrests you make and the more people you evaluate, the more weird things you will witness. It's called experience.

## PUPILARY REACTION

The eyes can't lie to you. If you listen to them, you'll have all of your answers. People can control their body movements. They can lie to you verbally and they can try to calm their respiration and breathing. They can try and conceal their breath with mints and gum. Smart tweakers take daily calcium vitamins to prevent their teeth from rotting out. They can wash their hair and try to look presentable. Some do it for court. Others don't care. But the one thing people cannot control to try to use and fool you is their pupil's reaction to light. If you learn how to read the pupils, you can determine if they just used or if they are coming down from a high. You can sometimes tell immediately if they have marijuana in their system or if they have used a stimulant. You can tell if they have used opiates or pain killers. And, you can tell if a person is a long time user. Here's how.

A normal pupil's diameter measures between 3.0mm to 6.5mm. Most officers carry a pupilometer with them and use it during their drug evaluations. If you don't have one, find one. If you find one, don't enlarge or reduce it while making a copy. They are pre measured circles to use for accurate drug evaluations. If you don't have a pen light, get one. I have used mini-mag flashlights, doctor's penlights, and every other small light source I could find. Don't use your million candle powered Surefire tactical light. It's too much light and not only can it harm the person's pupils, it might just piss him off and get you into a fight.

# REBOUND DILATION

In a dark area, ask the suspect to look at you. Take the light source and put it on his pupil. Watch to see how fasts it constricts. If it slams shut quickly, hold the light on it for several seconds and see if it starts to slowly dilate. If it does, and then goes back to its large diameter, there is dope on board. That person probably used several hours ago and isn't a long term user. They might have been using for only a few years. If the pupil's diameter is 6.5mm or more in darkness, they are probably new to the game. If you see this, it is called rebound dilation. It is indicative of meth or cocaine use and shows the person is still high, but coming down.

If the person's pupil is dilated and you shine your light on it and it moves ever so slightly, they probably used within an hour or two. You might not see the reaction to light, but there is always some movement. The only time a pupil doesn't react is in death. Try it. The next time you are sent to a dead body and you're waiting for homicide or the coroner to arrive, shine your light in the decedent's pupils. They won't react. If they do, cancel the coroner and start medical aid.

If a doper's pupils are constricted, don't automatically assume they're on heroin or some other narcotic. Long time meth users often have constricted pupils. It is more difficult to see rebound dilation, but if you check them in the dark and look closely, you'll see the slight movement or rebound dilation just as with a blown pupil. Most cranksters who use meth don't use heroin and vice versa. In the 1980s and into the 1990s, dopers would sometime mix heroin and real cocaine. Both drugs had natural ingredients and mixed well. It was called a "speed ball." The cocaine would speed them up and give them a good high and the opium from the heroin would stretch the high out over a longer period of time. Cocaine highs were short lived and the addicts were looking for something better and longer. They found it with cocaine base, or "rock cocaine" and later with crystal meth.

You don't see users mixing tar heroin and crystal meth too often. Although some still do. So if you see a constricted pupil with a tweaker, it'll likely be on one who is in his late thirties or older who has used for over twenty years. You can still see rebound dilation with them and make a very good guess.

## HIPPUS

Hippus is defined as the pulsation of the pupil. It is debatable as to what drugs cause hippus. In my experience, if I saw hippus, unequivocally, there was marijuana in the system. I never received a urine drug test back when I saw hippus during the drug evaluation and there was no THC in the person's system. Some officers I have spoken to believe methamphetamine alone can cause hippus, but I haven't experienced this myself.

My first year in patrol I kept a log of all the under-the-influence arrests I made. At the end of the year, I counted 75 arrests and my log included what drugs I suspected they had used and what drugs tested positive in their urine. I had mistakenly arrested five people for suspicion of methamphetamine use who tested positive only for marijuana. I reviewed my drug influence worksheets and saw they all showed hippus. I asked some drug experts in my department why I was seeing symptoms consistent with speed and the suspect's were testing positive only for marijuana. This is what I learned.

## MARIJUANA vs. METHAMPHETAMINE SYMPTOMS

In the 1970s, typical marijuana had a THC level of about three to six percent. Its effects were relatively slight and the typical "pot head" resembled characters like Cheech and Chong. Hash had a much higher THC level and was therefore more common than today. Marijuana is more scientifically researched and grown today resulting in a product with a THC content sometimes as high as fifteen to twenty percent. This high level of THC can cause effects similar to methamphetamine or speed use. Marijuana aficionados who subscribe to "High Times" and other publications and whose hobbies include the smoking and cultivation of marijuana, create incredibly high grade marijuana.

One night, two other deputies and I were using an informant to make controlled drug buys and after we successfully bought prescription pills from one dealer and methamphetamine from another, I asked the informant if he could buy from anyone else. The informant couldn't think of anyone and I asked him if he knew anybody who was selling marijuana. He said, "Oh, I thought you wanted to buy drugs. Sure, I know a guy who sells weed." It was almost an afterthought, but we gave the C.I. (confidential informant) fifty bucks and sent him into the house. He returned with some amazing marijuana that was so strong, we all nearly got hungry ourselves.

I wrote a search warrant on the marijuana house and a few days later, we served the warrant. It was very successful and we seized over thirty pounds of marijuana, guns, Oxycontin, and over fifteen thousand dollars in cash. The dealer was a marijuana hobbyist and had a very elaborate indoor and outdoor grow. I found the seeds he used and they were neatly packaged and named. The male seeds were in separate packages from the female seeds and when I interviewed him, I learned he was an amateur horticulturist and he liked creating new types of marijuana. He was proud to admit his marijuana had the highest level of THC he'd ever smoked and its reputation on the street among users was impressive.

Over the years, I have learned a couple symptoms to look for that help me determine if a person is under-the-influence of just marijuana, methamphetamine, or both. When I see all the symptoms of a central nervous system stimulant, i.e. an elevated pulse rate, a fast internal clock, eyelid and finger tremors, and dilated pupils, there are a couple of things I look for to see if there is marijuana on board. If I see hippus and not rebound dilation, I expect to find marijuana in the person's system and the first thing I look for to determine if there is only marijuana on board and not methamphetamine is convergence.

## CONVERGANCE

Converge is the following of the pupils on an object to the center where the eyes cross and maintain their position. When I conduct a thorough drug influence evaluation, I hold my ink pen about twelve inches in front of the person's face and I tell him to follow it with his eyes and not to move his head. I move the pen to the right slowly and then to the left looking for horizontal gaze nystagmus, or the involuntary jerking of the eyes. This is commonly used in drug evaluations and for determining a person's impairment from alcohol. Then, I move the pen in a circular motion and I bring it to the bridge of his nose and I hold it there for several seconds looking to see if he can follow it with his eyes and hold them on the pen. If his eyes stay focused on the pen after several seconds have passed and they stay crossed, this is convergence. If

I saw hippus, or the pulsating of the pupils, when I shined my penlight into his pupils and the eyes converge, I expect to find a stimulant in his system in addition to marijuana. If the eyes don't converge, it is called non-convergence.

## NON-CONVERGENCE

Non-convergence is also called a "lazy eye" and is a symptom of marijuana intoxication. I use this exam to eliminate the possibility of a stimulant in the system. If I have seen symptoms consistent with having recently used meth and when I check the pupils I see hippus, I check for non-convergence. I check the pupil's ability to follow my pen like I described above. If one of the eyes rolls off and fails to track the pen as I hold it at the nose, this is called non-convergence and I expect to find marijuana in the person's system. If the eyes cross and maintain, I expect to find meth in the person's system.

## OTHER SIGNS OF MARIJUANA INTOXICATION

As I mentioned before and will continue to say throughout this book, if I don't know an answer, I ask. One of the best ways to learn if a person has marijuana in their system is to ask him. Most dopers don't think of marijuana as an illegal drug and they are very open about their marijuana use. If you're not sure, ask your suspect when he last smoked marijuana. Usually, he will admit to having smoked some earlier in the day. This admission can help you better understand the signs and symptoms you are seeing during your drug evaluation.

Another good symptom you can look for to determine marijuana intoxication is by looking at the person's tongue. Sometimes, depending on when he smoked weed before you stopped him, his tongue might be coated with a brownish or greenish film. Most tweakers smoke cigarettes and you'll usually see a white, dehydrated coating on their tongue. A person who smokes marijuana might also have a white coated tongue if he used methamphetamine as well. When you're looking at the tongue, look on the backside of the tongue for small blisters. This is indicative of a smoker.

Years ago I used to smoke cigarettes and I never knew the damage I was causing my mouth and tongue. Of course, I knew the damage it caused my lungs and I knew smoking was the leading cause of heart disease. But, I didn't realize some of the other effects. One night I was showing a younger deputy what signs to look for during a drug evaluation. I had arrested a cooperative doper who didn't mind me teaching the youngster by showing him what symptoms I was using during my drug evaluation. I asked my suspect to stick his tongue out as far as he could and he did. I saw several small blisters on the back of his tongue and I showed them to the younger deputy. I told the deputy those blisters were caused from smoking crank. And, to some extent, I was right. But, I soon learned that a person could get those types of blisters by smoking anything, not just crank. Later that evening, I was using the restroom and I stuck my tongue out while I looked in the mirror and I was horrified when I saw that I too had the same types of blisters as the doper I arrested earlier. Within a few shorts months, I quit smoking.

Another sign that a person smokes marijuana is the smell. I doubt there is any law enforcement officer working patrol today who hasn't smelled marijuana or who wouldn't recognize it if they did. Marijuana has a very identifiable pungent odor when it is burning and like cigarette smoke, it stays in a person's hair and clothes. So, you can sometimes smell if a person has recently smoked marijuana. Think back to any concert or major sporting event you have attended. I would bet you smelled marijuana at some point during the show.

## URINE SAMPLE

There are some legal issues when obtaining a urine sample from your suspect. The bottom line is, you can only obtain a urine sample from a suspect in "a legally approved manner." The best advice I can give to overcome this barrier is to follow your department's policy and procedures pertaining to drug influence arrests and the seizing of a urine sample for evidence and drug analysis. The crime laboratory in my county tests urine samples for all the common drugs by testing the amount of nanograms in the urine. A nanogram is a unit of measurement that is one part per billion. Our laboratory has a scale they use to determine if the amount of the suspected drug is significant enough to show the sample tests positive for that drug.

All of this scientific garble is mostly unimportant to me. If the suspect is cooperative, I get a urine sample from him and I send it to the lab for urine drug analysis. It helps later in court to support my opinion the person was under-the-influence at the time I arrested him. If I arrest an uncooperative doper who refuses to provide a urine sample, I don't worry. I complete a thorough drug evaluation on him and I am confident I can prove, through my testimony, that he was under-the-influence of a certain drug at the time I arrested him. So don't put all of your emphasis on the urine sample. Use your training, your suspect's signs and symptoms, and your expertise first and a urine sample last. Remember, a urine result takes several weeks sometimes to return and you are going to take the person to jail based on your probable cause, not a urine drug result.

## COMPARISON EVALUATIONS

Like I mentioned earlier, the mindset you must have to be successful in working street-level dope is that everyone is under-the-influence unless they prove to you otherwise. If you evaluate every suspect you contact during all of your investigations and calls for service, in just a few months you should have a hundred drug evaluations under your belt. That doesn't mean you'll have a hundred arrests, because not everyone at the time of your evaluation will be high. Being able to describe a sober person's pupillary reaction to a light stimulus is just as important as knowing what rebound dilation and hippus mean. You must evaluate sober people to get a base or means to work from in establishing that a person is high.

Inevitably, you will find yourself on the witness stand in court someday and a defense attorney is going to ask you if you've ever met their client before. Most of the time, your answer will be, "No." They will elaborate and ask you a question like, "So, you've never done a drug evaluation on him before? Is that correct?" And what they are alluding to is that since you've never seen the suspect sober, you don't really know what he looks and acts like if he's high. Well, you can explain that although you've never done a drug evaluation on that particular person, you have conducted drug evaluations on people who you determined had not used drugs because of the normal results of your exam i.e. their pulse rate was normal, their pupils reacted to light and stayed constricted, they didn't have eyelid and finger tremors, they estimated thirty seconds in twenty-nine seconds, etc.

Being able to tell if a person is sober is just as important as being able to determine if a person is high. With practice and experience this will become second nature to you and you'll know when you need to evaluate someone for recent drug use. The more you see, the more experience you'll gain. Remember, these are things that help you develop your expertise in under-the-influence detection and it will help your confidence grow. With more confidence, you will become better and better at finding dopers and making arrests. And with this experience and very important tool in your war bag, you are in the process of becoming a good, well rounded, street-level dope cop.

# Chapter Four
## Surveillance

## FIXED SURVEILLANCE

Without a doubt, the best method of gathering firsthand intelligence on a drug location is by conducting your own surveillance. Once you learn about a possible drug house, find a place to sit and watch it. Drive around the area during your routine patrol and look for a concealed location where you can sit still and watch the house. Sometimes, you will have to park a few blocks away or over one block in an adjacent alley. If the house is in a trailer park you might have to drive along the outside fence, park your car, and stand up looking over the fence. Whether it is in an alley in a dark crevice, behind a semi truck parked on the street, or in an almond orchard, you must find a covert place to sit and watch. Be prepared to sit idle for at least thirty minutes to let everything settle after you arrive and start your surveillance.

My dad used to take me squirrel hunting when I was a kid. I remember walking through the woods and hearing the twigs and dry leaves crunching under my feet. My dad told me to find a spot, sit still, and listen. When I first found a fallen tree or stump to lean against, I listened and heard nothing. It seemed there were no animals within miles. After I sat completely still for ten or fifteen minutes and made no noise, the forest would come alive. I could hear a bird chirping in the distance followed by others. And then chipmunks would start scurrying around knocking leaves and debris from the trees. After all of the animals got comfortable with me being there, the squirrels would start to run again and bark. Within about twenty or thirty minutes, I could hear a squirrel bark in the distance followed by the answer from another. I learned then how to be still, watch, and listen. I used those lessons I learned hunting as a kid later when I became a cop and was conducting surveillance on dopers. After all, police work is sometimes like hunting and isn't man the most dangerous big game of all?

After I joined the infantry, I learned more about noise and light discipline. While I was at Fort Benning, Georgia, I remember my drill sergeant teaching us about how to stay concealed at night. During one particular exercise, we were all seated in bleachers looking out toward the darkness. About three hundred meters away was another drill sergeant with a hand held radio. My sergeant radioed to the sergeant down range and told him to light a cigarette. He did and even from that distance we could see the orange glow from the cigarette clearly enough to put our rifle sights on it and make an accurate shot. Then, the sergeant with the cigarette turned on his flashlight and began shining it around. Obviously, it was clearly visible and it gave his position away. He changed to a red lens on his flashlight and then we could barely see it glow. With the red lens he was still visible, but nowhere near as obvious as he was with the white lens on his flashlight. Next, he and another sergeant started talking to each other. If we listened closely, we could hear their voices. He locked the bolt on his rifle to the rear and let it slam forward. We heard the metallic clicking as it went forward. It was a wonderful demonstration of how easy it is to give yourself and your position away during darkness and I never forgot what I learned that night.

## NOISE AND LIGHT DISCIPLINE

Once you have found the best place to sit and watch a drug house you have to be aware of the noises you make and the light you use. I recall watching a particular house one summer night. I was driving a spare patrol car because my assigned car was in the shop for service.

The radio and traffic advisor console in this car was completely different from mine. I was sitting with the windows rolled down and the engine off. I was probably too close to the house I was watching. I saw a bicyclist ride up to the house and my target came outside and was talking to him on the front porch. The radio was a little too loud and I reached down instinctively to turn it down. When I did, I accidentally hit the passenger side spotlight turning it on and it shined right on the house, my target, and the bicyclist. I burned myself and that house for several weeks. I was unfamiliar with the location of the equipment and a simple mistake like that cost me. With my light shined on them, they stood there looking at me and all I could do was wave "hello" and drive away feeling stupid.

Some car radios don't turn down all the way and even on their lowest volume setting, they're too loud. Many times, I would turn the car radio off and listen with my hand held radio. It could be adjusted better and if I thought it was too loud, I would put a piece of black electrical tape over the speaker to muffle it even more. Today, there are earpiece microphones that connect to your hand held radio and bypass the lapel microphone completely. If you can stand having something in your ear all night, go for it. Personally, I don't like having a microphone stuck in my ear and I use tape over my speaker. Whatever you choose, be aware your police radio is a dead give away when you are trying to be quiet and use stealth to conduct surveillance.

Another common mistake I see uniformed officers make when they are trying to be inconspicuous is they turn on their interior dome light. Most patrol cars can de-activate the dome lights so they don't come on when you open your car door. If you can't turn off your car's interior dome light, remove the bulb. If you don't want to do that, buy a pair of spring clips that hold the buttons down simulating the doors being closed. I have a pair I bought from Quadratec for about ten dollars I use on my Jeep when I drive with the doors removed. Be conscious of the light you use when you are close to a drug house conducting surveillance. If you need to use light, put your hand over your flashlight lens to dim the light as much as possible. If you have one, use a red lens over your flashlight or interior dome light. Don't use your spotlights, alley lights, or take-down lights. I know it's hard to leave all those switches and buttons alone when you are sitting there bored, but if you want to be effective you will have to be disciplined. It isn't easy. That's why it's called "noise and light discipline."

## LET YOUR EYES ADJUST

Whether you are sitting in your car or doing foot patrols at night, give your eyes time to adjust to the darkness. It takes about twenty minutes for your eyes to develop their full night vision. If you allow them to adjust to the dark, you'll be amazed at how well you can see at night without using light. If you let your eyes adjust and then blast your bazillion candle power flashlight at every little noise, nook, and cranny, you have not only announced your presence to every tweaker and criminal within a mile, you have killed your night vision and when you turn off your light, you wont be able to see anything.

A trick I learned as an infantryman is to close your dominant eye if you are going to be exposed to light. We learned this as soldiers when moving at night and trip flares were fired into the air. We were taught to close our dominant eye until the light passed so our night vision wasn't lost. I used this same technique when conducting surveillance at night. If I was sitting in my car and another car shined its headlights in my direction, I would close one and sometimes both of my eyes until the headlights passed. That helped me keep my night vision and be able to see after I was exposed to the light. If I needed to use my flashlight to find something or write notes, I closed my dominant eye and did whatever I needed to do with my left eye.

Using these techniques takes time to get used to. It is something different and it takes practice to make them second nature. You must be thinking all the time you are conducting surveillance from a marked patrol car. You must be aware of how much noise your car is making. Lower the radio and make sure it isn't too loud. Be aware of your lights and how you use them. More often than not, being completely blacked-out is the safest way to hide at night. There are times to use your lights, but usually during surveillance you want to remain dark and quiet.

## CONCEALMENT

Concealing yourself while you are in a marked patrol car is difficult at times, but it can be done. When you are looking for a place to watch a drug house, look for naturally dark areas. Use shadows to your advantage and try to imagine if you were standing at your dealer's house looking outward. Could you see yourself if you were looking in your direction? If so, then make adjustments and corrections. Look for natural concealment like shrubs and trees. Sometimes, you can park in a line of cars on the street facing your target house and blend in. Use whatever means you can to try and be concealed. If a good surveillance location is in the carport of a vacant house but the house has motion lights or a porch light shining all the time, unscrew the bulb while you are there. Be creative and think "outside the box." Of course, if you unscrew a light bulb or something to someone's house, be sure you restore it to however it was before you leave.

I was watching a drug house in a rural area one night and I was sitting across an open field at the edge of an almond orchard facing the house. I was invisible to the house until a car arrived. The cars would drive around the side of the house and turn down a long dirt road. Inevitably, every time a car arrived, I was completely illuminated and anyone looking in my direction could see the headlights reflect off my car's windshield. To avoid this reflection, I grabbed of couple of army green wool disaster blankets my department issued us. I draped the blankets over my hood, windshield, and top to prevent the light from reflecting back to the house. Then, I sat in the driver's seat and watched the house with my binoculars and looked through a small slit in the windshield where the two blankets met. I did this every time I got myself into position to watch that house and I never gave myself away. I got many good felony arrests from stops I made leaving there.

## BINOCULARS

A good pair of binoculars is one the best tools you can have when conducting surveillance from a fixed position. If you know how to use them properly, binoculars are very effective even at night. When I was doing some research before I bought a large caliber hunting rifle, I remember reading an article that read, "Buy a good rifle and spend as much money as you can on your scope." Good "glass" or binoculars will pay for themselves time and time again. I splurged a bit and bought a pair of Leopold Wind River compact binoculars. They were just over four hundred dollars, but their quality was well worth the investment.

I tried several different pairs until I finally paid the money and bought the Leopold's. I tried Bushnell, Tasco, and a friend's pair of Zeiss binoculars. The Zeiss outperformed in every way possible. But, I couldn't afford the thousand dollars they cost. I found the Leopold's for a somewhat affordable price. The difference between the lower end binoculars and the mid level Leopold's I bought was amazing. When you use binoculars at night, you'll see what I mean. The cheaper Tasco and Bushnell binoculars didn't focus completely and they were grayish and a little blurry. I couldn't read license plate numbers with clarity and when I looked through them for longer periods of time, my eyes got sore and I would sometimes get headaches from straining to focus my eyes. With the Leopold binoculars I eventually bought, I could read license numbers, street signs, and addresses crystal clear and I could conduct surveillance for hours without getting tired.

## HOW TO USE BINOCULARS

Most people grab a pair of binoculars and throw them up to their eyes expecting to see perfectly with no bouncing, blurring, or movement. Well folks, this isn't Hollywood and what you see through the sniper's scope on television isn't reality. There is a technique to using binoculars and getting them focused and adjusted properly. I wear glasses now and when I put binoculars to my eyes, I remove my glasses. Then, I close my left eye and focus the right lens of the binoculars until I can see as clearly as possible with my right eye only. This right lens adjustment is on the right tube of the binoculars near the eyepiece. Once my right lens is focused, I open my left eye and look through the binoculars with both eyes open. I then use the center adjustment on the binoculars to focus my left eye. Next, I open or close the binoculars so the "double vision" disappears. Once they are adjusted properly there should be only one field of view looking through the lenses toward your target. If I have a means available, I support the binoculars keeping them as steady as possible. When I am sitting in my car, I rest the binoculars on the steering wheel and they are solid and don't move. If I am standing, I lock my elbows into my chest making a somewhat stable platform to hold the binoculars up to my eyes.

## MOBILE SURVEILLANCE

After I worked an area for awhile, I usually knew about eight to ten drug houses in my beat. My normal practice when I just started my shift was to drive around and patrol check every dope house I knew. I would drive by and see if there were any cars parked in front I didn't recognize and if there were, I would write down the license plate numbers and find out who was driving those cars. I looked for any type of activity from that house. I didn't stop anything yet; I just conducted some mobile surveillance so I knew where I wanted to hunt later. This technique has proven effective in every assignment I have worked. If my shift started during daylight and then continued into the evening, I took advantage of the daytime to better see the drug houses and I looked for things I couldn't normally see at night. During the daytime, I would drive by a drug house and look for video surveillance cameras hanging near the front door and mounted under the eaves. These types of things were difficult to see at night and daytime was the perfect time to get this intelligence.

## FOOT SURVEILLANCE

Many times, there was no way to effectively watch a drug house from a patrol car and I did my surveillance on foot. I tried to do this kind of surveillance with a partner, but if I didn't have one, I went alone. The first thing I would do before I started walking was jump up and down and listen for the noises I made. If my keys rattled, I took them off my belt. Sometimes, I would leave my keys in my car and only take my car key with me. I'd put that in my pocket so it wasn't banging around on my belt. Nearly every time I checked myself for noise by jumping up and down, my handcuffs shook in their cases. I would take them out and open them up wider so the friction in the case kept them still. If my baton slapped against my radio, I carried it in my hand. Whatever made noise, I fixed.

I made sure my cell phone was on vibrate. There was nothing worse than standing five feet away from a drug house, looking through the slats on a fence, and having your cell phone ring. I always carried my cell phone with me, but left it on silent. After I fixed all of my noise problems, I made sure my radio volume was low and that the speaker was covered with electrical tape. Then, I would grab my spare flashlight.

It never failed, I always got myself into something when I was away from my patrol car and my flashlight died. If I was wearing my tactical uniform with cargo pockets, I would drop my digital camera in one pocket just in case I needed to take a photograph of a car or house. Sometimes, depending on what I was doing and how far I was going to be from my target house, I would hang my binoculars around my neck just in case.

Whether I was working alone or with a partner, I always telephoned my dispatch and told them where I was going to be on foot patrol. If I was alone, I didn't go on foot to make arrests. I used my foot patrols to conduct close surveillance and gather intelligence. I only made arrests when I was on foot if I had to. My goal, exclusively, was to be undetected and to watch. Like in my car, on foot I used darkness and anything available as concealment. Naturally, it was easier to get closer to a dope house on foot than in a patrol car and you saw things differently the closer you got. The importance of having good noise and light discipline magnified ten fold when on foot and was more critical than when sitting blocks away in a car.

## SURVEILLANCE TO CONTACT

The purpose of surveillance is to gather firsthand intelligence you can use to make stops and get good felony arrests. When you are watching a house either on foot or in your car, you have to put yourself in a position where you can leave your hiding place and make a stop. If you are working alone, it is more difficult to watch a house from a concealed location and then make a stop on a vehicle leaving. It can be done, however you just have to be cognizant of this fact when you find your surveillance location. Know that you must be able to watch the house, see a person or car leave, and then put yourself in a position to follow them and make a stop.

If you have a partner, this isn't a problem. When I had a partner who wanted to hunt and work street-level dope with me, we took turns watching houses and calling out stops. I would tell my partner when a car arrived and left and then let him make the stop. Then, I would carefully leave my surveillance position, to avoid giving myself away to the dealer, and go back him up on the stop. If we got a hook great! Once he was done booking his arrest, he would sit at the surveillance spot and call out stops for me. We did this all night long until we got tired of hunting a particular house. If I was watching a dope house and saw a car arrive, I watched to see who got out of the car and went into the house or made contact with the dealer. I was usually able to tell my partner how many people were in the car, which one bought the dope, what type of car they drove, and if there were any inoperable lights or equipment violations he could use to stop the car when it left.

However you choose to work your surveillance and watch drug houses, remember the ultimate goal is to watch a drug transaction and then make a stop on the suspect leaving that house. By using surveillance and the techniques I described, and if you are patient enough to sit still and watch, your pendulum of *Luck vs. Skill* will be turned in your favor so much there will be little luck involved in the arrests you make. The volume and quality of your arrests will improve significantly and your supervisors and partners are definitely going to notice your productivity increase. And, you will have a sense of satisfaction and pride knowing you are using your skills to make the arrests and those arrests are going to positively impact the community you serve.

# chapter Five
# The Arrest And Evidence Collection

## TO ARREST OR NOT

Early one morning, I was working patrol and stopped a black guy who I knew from prior contacts. The guy was riding his bicycle with a basket attached to the front. I stopped him for riding his bike at night without a light. He was tall and skinny and was nearly fifty-years-old. I had stopped him probably five times before and I knew he was a meth user. But, I never had any problems with him before. It was my Friday and I didn't want to create any unnecessary work for myself. After I talked to him for about ten minutes or so, I decided to let him go. About two hours later, I was sent to a burglary report at the Elk's Lodge. The lodge was about three blocks from where I stopped the guy on the bicycle earlier. The back door had been kicked open and food and liquor was stolen.

Every year, the Elk's Lodge bought hamburgers and hotdogs to cook lunch at the local elementary school. Later that day, they were going to cook lunch for the kids. Everyone in town knew what they did and therefore everyone knew there were frozen hamburger patties and hotdogs stored there. I took the report and processed the scene for evidence. I lifted a print off the freezer door and started talking to neighbors looking for a witness or additional evidence. The Fire Department was across the street and I spoke with a fireman. He told me he saw a tall skinny black male riding a bicycle, with a basket attached to the front, leaving the alley from the back of the Elk's Lodge around the time of the burglary. He saw what looked to him like hamburger buns stored in the basket on the front of the bike.

I went to the office and made a photo-line up of the black guy I had spoken with earlier that morning and showed it to the fireman. He identified my suspect as the person he saw leaving the Elk's Lodge. I wrote a search warrant for the suspect's house and later that morning, I searched his house, but didn't find the food items. I knew he burglarized the Elk's Lodge, but I couldn't prove it. The fingerprint later returned to a club member who bought the hamburgers the day before and put the food in the refrigerator. My suspect denied any involvement in the burglary and the case went unsolved. I ended up working about eight hours over my normal shift, did a lot of work, and came up empty handed. The bottom line is I should have arrested the guy on the bicycle earlier that morning for being under-the-influence and I would have prevented a burglary, saved the Elk's Lodge hundreds of dollars, allowed the kids to enjoy their special yearly treat, and I would have saved myself a huge amount of work and overtime that produced nothing.

As I have mentioned before and will continue to reiterate throughout this book, when you are developing your skills as a street-level dope cop, you must arrest everyone who is under-the-influence every chance you get. Everyone is under-the-influence of drugs until they prove to you otherwise. The only way they can prove to you they are sober is by allowing you to perform an under-the-influence evaluation on them. Once you start evaluating hundreds of people for being under-the-influence, you will start to become an expert at detecting deception and finding the truth. Once you become an expert at this, you will start to make more and more arrests. Then, and only then, can you start to choose which ones go to jail and which ones don't.

After I made a couple hundred under-the-influence arrests, I started a game when dealing with dopers. I started only arresting the ones who lied to me. If I stopped someone and he was honest with me and told me he used recently and I didn't think he was a burglar and would later cause problems if I released him, I offered to let him go in exchange for some information. The information didn't always involve drugs. Sometimes, if I was looking for a warrant suspect or stolen property, I would ask the person about that. If he gave me something I thought was credible, I let him go. Of course, if my area was being burglarized regularly, then everyone went to jail. And usually, the burglaries stopped.

Then, when I found a die hard who just would not admit to using drugs when I knew, in fact, he had, I would arrest him. If he changed his tune later at the office and started telling me the truth, I would tell him if he had just been honest with me up front, he wouldn't have been arrested. This game was especially fun when I stopped a group of people. The ones who were honest walked away. The ones who were not, I arrested. It was a type of psychological warfare, I suppose, but it was effective. It challenged me to use my skills in determining if someone had recently used drugs when he was adamant he had not. Then, I would keep track of those arrests and check myself against the urine results if one was provided. It might seem mean or pointless, but it kept my skills sharp and I continued to learn and develop as a street-level dope cop. Then, after I had done this routine on dopers countless times, everyone started telling me the truth. I remember asking a doper one time, "When was the last time you used?" He said, "I'm not going to lie to you man. I smoked some about an hour ago." When I arrested him, he said, "You can't arrest me. I told you the truth!"

One thing I learned from the volume of stops and arrests I made was how to use my skills and intelligence I had gathered to know when to not arrest someone. That sounds strange and contradictory after I have preached everyone goes to jail, but there are times when you will start to catch and release.

## CATCH AND RELEASE

After you have become an expert at making under-the-influence arrests, it is time to move forward and start making possession arrests. You will know when it's time to graduate. Your confidence level will be high and you'll likely have a reputation amongst the criminals as being aggressive. When you reach that point, you will have to start letting people go in order to make more possession arrests. It is like fishing.

The fisherman in search of a trophy fish catches a bunch of small pan fish. He keeps casting his line and reeling in the fish. He does this until he catches "a keeper" or a "big fish." Tweakers are like fish. When you catch one and he is under-the-influence, you can arrest him and spend two hours doing an under-the-influence worksheet, transport, and booking papers, or you can cut him loose and try to find another one who is in possession of dope. Eventually, you'll start to arrest more and more people for felony possession and you won't waste time with misdemeanors unless a person is causing problems and needs to go to jail. In my opinion, you reach this point after you have made a hundred or more under-the-influence arrests.

Part of the catch and release practice involves using the information you have gathered from informants, other intelligence, and your surveillance. Many times, informants will tell you users know you are watching a particular house. This will either deter them from buying at that house or they will take the time and effort to hide their dope before they move. This makes your job much harder and you are losing the battle in the *Luck vs. Skill* pendulum. When you are watching a dope house, there will be times when you need to let a car come and go untouched. If you stop and arrest everyone leaving a drug house, you will dry up your fishing hole. If that is your goal, then go forth and conquer. If not, back off and let some go. There are times when you need to let them deal and get comfortable with their transactions. Comfortable dopers are careless dopers and you are more likely to catch one carrying dope in his coin pocket if he feels confident he won't be stopped.

When I was a young man in the Army going through infantry school, I remember learning about the ambush. I learned that when setting up an ambush on an enemy patrol, you always let the patrol walk into your ambush and get about halfway through before you opened fire and killed everyone. The reason was simple. If you shot the point man as soon as he walked into the ambush, the rest of the patrol would take cover and return fire. You could kill more if you let the first few walk into an ambush kill zone and get comfortable before opening fire.

Hunting dopers sometimes is the same. Your goal is to keep them off balance. Their job is to get away with using and selling dope and your job is to catch them. Sometimes you hit them hard and fast and other times you let them go. Big game trophy hunters epitomize this concept. A hunter who pays a lot of money for a trophy will let smaller game pass in front of his sights. He waits until the right one comes along. Then, he fires his shot. Once you have graduated from under-the-influence arrests, you want to become a big game hunter. You want to focus on getting possession arrests.

After you begin making several possession arrests, it is natural to move toward larger quantities and start arresting dealers. Dealers should be your ultimate target. It is a simple matter of supply and demand. If you take out the distributors, the supply will be diminished. If you take out a drug house in a particular neighborhood, chances are the property crimes occurring around that house will disappear. Take notice the next time you arrest someone for possession for sales. Read the reports and see how many property crimes were reported in the neighborhood where the dealer's house was located. Then, go back a month or two and see how many reports were taken before you made that arrest. You will see the difference. And you will know you have made the difference from your pro-active on-sight arrests.

## EVIDENCE COLLECTION

I heard a deputy tell me once that he liked arresting tweakers because there was no evidence to collect and the reports were short. I thought how mistaken that deputy was and I felt sorry for him when he went to court. There is plenty of evidence you can seize and use during simple under-the-influence arrests. Obviously, you can get a urine sample from your suspect. But, there is much more. How often do you find spent baggies on someone you stop and arrest for being under-the-influence? True, an empty baggie by itself is insignificant. But, that baggie in the possession of a person who is high is excellent circumstantial evidence.

I was on the stand testifying once during a suppression motion. I had arrested a guy in a vacant house for possession. The guy had an outstanding warrant for his arrest. When I arrested him, I found a loaded syringe in his pocket. I evaluated him to see if he was under-the-influence and he wasn't. So, I didn't charge him for being high.

Later in court, the defense attorney asked me if his client was under-the-influence and I said, "No." The attorney acted dumbfounded that a person was in possession of a loaded syringe and wasn't high. I laughed to myself and told the attorney that if I had found an empty syringe in his pocket, I would expect him to be high. If the syringe was full, it meant he hadn't used it yet and I would expect him to be sober! The judge nodded his head agreeing with me and basically told the defense attorney his question was stupid.

## SPENT BINDLES AND MISC PAPERS

After that experience in court, I began seizing empty bindles and baggies as evidence in simple under-the-influence investigations. An empty baggie is good evidence of drug use. It can easily be argued a normal person who doesn't use drugs isn't going to have empty baggies in his pocket, wallet, or purse. Once I started to look for evidence, I started finding papers in doper's pockets and wallets with the names of other drug users and dealers. I would go through a person's phone book and cell phone to look for names I recognized and if I found ones I knew from prior investigations were involved in drug activity, I would seize those items as evidence. Then, I would copy those names and numbers to use later during other drug investigations. It was powerful evidence to seize and document in your report the person you arrested for suspicion of being under-the-influence of drugs had, in his possession, the name and phone number of a known drug dealer.

## GLASS PIPES

When I first started working patrol in the late nineties, it was common practice for cops to find a doper in possession of a crank pipe. Nine times out of ten, the deputy would smash the pipe on the ground and let the person go. I used to do this myself until I actually looked inside a pipe one day and saw a huge glob of crank melted in the bottom. I used a paperclip and scraped nearly two grams of meth from the pipe. Suddenly, that simple misdemeanor paraphernalia became a good felony possession arrest. I later spoke to the doper in possession of that "loaded" pipe and he told me everyone was carrying their dope melted inside their pipes because they knew what the cops would do if they found it. Inevitably, the cops would break the pipe on the ground and destroy evidence of a felony! Well, since then, every time I find a pipe I look to see how much dope is melted inside. If there is enough dope to be considered a "useable amount," I use a paperclip and scrape the dope into an empty plastic Ziploc bag and I send it to the lab for analysis. Then, I book the pipe and paperclip as evidence of possession.

## PHOTOGRAPHS

One year my wife asked me what I wanted for Christmas. I was working in a rural substation and was making countless under-the-influence arrests. Technology hadn't yet found its way to my substation. We had one 35mm camera there we could use for major crimes. That depended, of course, on whether or not you knew how to use a box camera with an ISO/ASA setting and adjust the depth of field on the lens and the shutter speed. Digital cameras were outrageously expensive and we had to document the use of film and send it to our lab for processing. I had no way to photograph people I had arrested. Booking photos were kept downtown and it was a chore to review them. So, I told my wife I wanted a Polaroid camera. Santa Claus delivered and I became a photo junkie. My department supplied us film for Polaroids and I soon had a photo album of local crooks I had arrested.

Since then, technology has progressed and now we all have digital cameras assigned. Now, I photograph everything! Remember the old saying, "A picture is worth a thousand words?" I take photos of the tweaker to show his oily skin and dilated pupils. If I seize baggies or crank pipes, I photograph those as well. I take pictures of everything to document what I saw and seized. It might seem excessive to some, but in my opinion, it shows the attorneys, your supervisors, your partners, and the crooks that you are very thorough and competent.

One evening, I was watching a dope house and I saw an old truck drive down the alley and stop in front of the house. It was night time and I was watching the house with my binoculars. I saw a ball hitch attached to the truck's rear bumper blocked the middle number of the license plate. The truck left a few minutes later and I followed it. I couldn't read the middle number still, so I made a traffic stop on the truck for an obstructed plate. When I radioed the stop to dispatch, I told them the plate was obstructed.

I later arrested the driver for driving on a suspended license. During an inventory search of the truck before the tow's arrival, I found three ounces of meth on the driver's seat. I charged the guy for transportation for sales. Using my digital camera, I took a photograph of the ball hitch attached to the rear bumper obstructing the plate. I took the first photograph standing at the rear passenger side of his truck looking downward. From that angle, the numbers on the plate were clearly visible. I decided to take another picture from a different angle. This time, I sat in my driver's seat and took the picture looking through my front windshield facing the truck. This was the same view I had when I was driving behind. It was this view which gave me the probable cause to stop the truck in the first place. From that angle, the plate was obstructed and I couldn't read the middle number.

He had prior drug sales offenses, had been to prison before, and was facing five years in prison for transportation for sales. He was desperate to get the charges dismissed. He claimed I made an illegal stop and lied about my probable cause for stopping him. Later at court during a suppression hearing, he produced a photograph of his license plate and bumper. Amazingly, the hitch was now attached to the bumper upside-down and nothing blocked the numbers on the plate. Well, the suspect felt pretty good about himself until the district attorney reminded him and his counselor I took a couple of pictures of the hitch myself that night at the scene before I towed his truck. The photos clearly showed an obstructed plate and a vehicle code violation. The sigh of air leaving the guy said it all. He knew he was done. He pled to possession for sales and was sentenced to five years in prison. I hope all is well and he gets along with his cell mate.

In the earlier chapter where I discussed making traffic stops, I mentioned different violations you can use as your probable cause. If you can, make a stop for a violation you can photograph. In this case, had I made a stop for a moving violation, I would have had no physical evidence to prove the violation. I still might have won the argument in court, but I could just have easily lost and a drug dealer could have walked free. It is situations like these that give you experience. These experiences are what you use to change how you do business. You continue to learn and get better. Your expertise doesn't end when you reach a certain level of competence. You continue to learn and make mistakes. From those mistakes you get better and learn and your partners learn and improve their skills. And as time passes you get more proficient. This is the process of becoming an expert. And it is great fun winning battles in court and sending bad guys to jail.

## RECORDING YOUR INTERVIEW

Technology has progressed so fast the days of cassette tapes are over. If you don't have a digital recorder with a USB connector you can attach and download into a computer, go buy one. For about fifty dollars and a trip to Radio Shack, you can have one of the greatest tools you will ever own. A digital recorder is a superb tool for evidence collection. It is only limited to how creative you are and it can be used in so many applications. I have never regretted recording a phone call or interview. Being able to play back with digital clarity what happened and what was said has benefited me time and time again.

I began recording interviews after I was assigned to a substation and worked for a veteran sergeant who just finished a tour working as a homicide detective. He was such a believer in the value of evidence and the recorder as a means of collecting evidence, he purchased digital recorders for all of his deputies in that substation. Like most, I was reluctant to use the recorder at first and thought I didn't need one. I was guilty of thinking I didn't need to record my interviews because I could write down in my report what was said. Well, that's true to a point. But, once I started recording all of my interviews and I played them back before writing my reports, I learned there was a lot of useful information said during the interviews I wasn't including in my reports because by the time I spoke with someone for an hour, I couldn't remember every question I asked nor the answer given.

Once I started recording my interviews, even on misdemeanor under-the-influence investigations, I began to get praise from district attorneys for my thoroughness. One DA told me he was able to plea my cases out sometimes and keep me from having to testify because I recorded the interviews and listed that evidence in my report. I would download the recordings onto a compact disc and book the disc as evidence. The DA told me just the thought of presenting that recording of the interview as evidence, sometimes caused the defendants to plea. That was fine with me because I worked nights mostly and if I had a subpoena for court, I would get very little or no sleep sitting there. And,

I still had to work that night despite spending the day in court. Even worse, I would lose my days off sitting in court. Anything I could do to keep from having to go to court and testify was worthwhile to me.

Whether it is an empty baggie, a urine sample, a photograph, or a recording, evidence is powerful and should be collected and used whenever you can find it. Don't be the lazy, useless officer who doesn't want to collect or find evidence because it makes the report longer and takes more time. Be thorough and make every effort to find evidence, book it, and list it in your report. Eventually, you'll get used to doing good and thorough investigations and it will become second nature. When you normally do very good police work on smaller misdemeanor cases, you won't have any trouble at all when the time comes for you to use all of your advanced skills on a major case. Whether you are working street-level dope or just handling calls and investigating a petty theft, be thorough and seek to find and collect evidence. Eventually, your work will pay off and be noticed.

# Chapter Six
# The Confidential Informant

## INFORMANT TYPES

After I had been working patrol for about five or six years, I started to hone my skills as a street-level dope cop and as a police officer in general. I began to master my "Verbal Judo," as George Thompson called it, and I was learning how to investigate and document very thoroughly. But most importantly, I started to learn how to use my interpersonal communication skills to avoid citizen complaints and I began to get regular laudatories in my personal file. When I learned how to talk to people, I developed a pool of informants who kept me posted daily on not only drug activity, but criminal activity in general. With the amount of regular information I had at my disposal, there weren't too many problems or crimes I couldn't solve. And, when I worked with one or two other deputies who had their own information network and we compared notes and intelligence, we truly monopolized the townships we patrolled. Our bosses knew it, we knew it, and most importantly the criminals knew it. Within a couple of months, we could literally clean up an area so well, we could go days without a call for service. The bulk of the information we used came from the citizen informant.

## CITIZEN INFORMANT

A person who calls dispatch and tells us there is a warrant suspect hiding at a house is actually a citizen informant. Any information we receive from a person who is not under arrest and who is not giving us information with the expectation of getting something in return is categorized as a citizen informant. We can use information an anonymous reporting party gives us, within limits, and this person can be considered an informant. Naturally, we aren't typically going to write a search warrant and kick in a door from anonymous information. We can, however, use the anonymous information as a nexus to begin an investigation and later develop probable cause for a search warrant. The citizen informant is mostly honest and sincere, although typically their information is second hand and not as accurate as a criminal who is directly involved. It is our job as investigators to piece the information together and fill in the gaps to get the truth. Here's an example.

The grandmother who calls to report her granddaughter is using drugs isn't likely to know who is selling her granddaughter drugs. She will probably be able to tell you some of her granddaughter's associates. She might suspect one of her granddaughter's friends as being the drug dealer. But, she doesn't really know. She might tell you that person is selling drugs, but it is up to you to use your other intelligence to determine the validity. The grandmother might be giving you the names of other users and not dealers. The granddaughter, on the other hand, knows who is selling drugs and she is more likely to know the connection between her user friends, thieves, a dealer's house, a location of stolen property, etc. The grandmother's information isn't useless; it just isn't as complete as she thinks. Pieced together with other information you have it is valuable nonetheless and you can use it to help make arrests and solve crimes and community problems.

## CONFIDENTIAL INFORMANT

Cops love to toss around the phrase C.I. or "confidential informant." I chuckle every time I hear some rookie who has been on the streets for a month or two talk about his C.I. and so on. He thinks a person who tells him something is a confidential informant. To an extent, I suppose it is true. But, for the purposes of working street-level dope and developing and maintaining informants, when I refer to the confidential informant, I mean a suspect who has been arrested, signed a contract to provide information or conduct controlled drug buys, for the purposes of case leniency. When I refer to a C.I., I am not referring necessarily to a reporting party of a crime. If I am using a citizen informant on a regular basis and that person's information has led to successful arrests, then I might consider them a non-contractual confidential informant. For the most part, I am referring to the C.I. as a person whom I have arrested and am using to make other more significant arrests while that person is "working off" a case.

## CASE LENIENCY vs. MONETARY

A person who is arrested on an open offense and who is providing services or information with the intent of staying out of jail and not being charged is working under the promise of case leniency. For the uniformed patrol officer, this is the type of informant you will be working. As you advance in your ability to manage and use informants, you might start to pay them for controlled buys and other information. This, however, isn't typically done at the patrol level. Mercenaries, or paid informants, are more commonly found in major violator units. Whichever your department utilizes, make sure your boss is agreeable to your use of informants and has given you permission to use them. I'll cover this more when I discuss the informant contract later.

## PROVEN RELIABLE INFORMANT

Any informant who gives you information you can later prove accurate and that you use to make a successful arrest is considered a proven reliable informant. If a citizen informant, whose identity is known, tells you someone has dope in a certain location in their house and you are able to conduct a lawful search of that house, seize dope where the informant said it would be, and make an arrest, that informant has proven to be reliable. The same goes for a confidential informant. If you conduct a successful controlled drug buy, that person is now proven reliable. Now, when that person gives you information, it can be weighed as more credible than information given to you from someone who is unproven. This becomes important when you later write search warrants and the probable cause you are using is partially developed from a proven reliable informant.

# DEVELOPING THE INFORMANT

After you have begun to make more and more dope arrests and your confidence level has grown, it is likely you have arrested people who offered to give you information and who tried to get themselves out of going to jail by giving you that information. These people were potential informants. I am not a proponent of deputies using informants when they are completely new to working street-level dope. In fact, I think it is best that you focus on mastering your basic skills like making good stops and learning how to make solid under-the-influence arrests before trying to work informants. Eventually, you will have the confidence and tools you need to effectively develop and maintain confidential informants.

Although I have before, I don't usually make stops with the intention of arresting someone to use as an informant. Normally, when I am conducting an interview of a person I just arrested for an open drug charge, I get a sense of the person's character and by using interview and interrogation techniques, like asking baseline and elimination questions, I know with a degree of certainty, the person's level of honesty. I develop rapport with the person and determine if his personality and mine are compatible. If I think he might make a good confidential informant, I ask a series of questions to see if he meets my department's criteria.

# CRITERIA

If you work for a modern, contemporary department, there is a good chance you already have an informant management handbook or policy. If you do, great! Follow your policy and your agency's criteria for working an informant. Your department policy should govern the use of informants and give you the parameters they want you to use and work within. Those boundaries are usually established from experience and are there to keep you out of trouble. If you already have a working policy in place, read it, follow it, and make yourself an expert on it before you try to work a confidential informant. If you don't have a policy, here are some basic guidelines you can use to help you increase your success and avoid problems.

# CRIMINAL HISTORY

I was working an overtime shift one night in a substation I had worked before for three years. I was working with a newer deputy who complained he and his partners couldn't seem to find any dope. I didn't sign up for the overtime shift to get myself into any long drawn out investigations or tragedies, so I told the deputy we could find some dope and get a possession arrest if he wanted to write the paper. He was agreeable and I hopped in his passenger seat. Within about an hour, I saw a guy hiding next to a parked car when we drove by. We stopped and checked him. He was high and on probation for drugs. We searched him and found a couple of grams of meth and two crank pipes. I was satisfied and we arrested the guy for possession, being high, and the paraphernalia.

We drove him back to the substation and completed our investigation there. He told us he could buy dope from another guy and he gave us the dealer's name. We learned the dealer was a parolee at large and our suspect volunteered to set up a "road burn" (discussed later.) I checked our suspect for wants and warrants. Our computer link to NCIC was down and I could only check him locally. After he returned clear locally, we signed him up as a confidential informant and tried the "road burn." He called the dealer and was unsuccessful getting him to bring an ounce into town that night. We released the guy with his promise to set it up in a couple of days. The next morning, our computer link was working again and I learned our new C.I. had a no bail warrant out of Texas for manufacturing meth. Well, he disappeared and I spent nearly two months tracking him down before I arrested him for our case and the Texas warrant. This is what I learned.

When you find someone you think has good information and you want to work him, run his rapsheet and see what types of convictions he has. Don't just limit your rapsheet to your state. Run a full FBI rapsheet on him and look for out of state arrests and convictions as well. Check your database for local arrests that didn't result in a conviction that might not show on a rapsheet. If your suspect has a long history of crimes of violence, such as ADW and domestic assaults, don't use him. If he is on active parole or wanted, don't use him. If the person is a juvenile, don't use him. Think about it, would you actually send in a juvenile to buy dope? You are looking for a person who has only minor arrests and convictions. Remember, you are doing him a favor by signing him up as an informant and giving him the chance to work off a case. Also, you are using him as a uniformed patrol officer. You don't have the time and resources a specialized unit does to manage informants. Keep yours simple and safe. Also, don't consider using an informant to work off a crime involving a victim.

For example, let's say you arrest a suspect for burglary and he wants to give you information about the location of stolen property or a drug dealer for case leniency. You are not in a position to work him. There is a victim, other than the state, and your responsibility is to the victim of that crime, not to use their suspect to make a better arrest elsewhere. Don't use those types of crimes and suspects for case leniency. The types of cases you should use at first are misdemeanor drug charges you created from on-sight activity. Let someone work off an under-the-influence arrest or possession of drug paraphernalia at first. Then, if you are successful, you can start to use felony possessions if your department policy and supervisor permit.

## THE CONTRACT

The informant contract is very simple but important. It should list the case number of the offense the informant wants work off and the reason. I write a very brief paragraph that details what I want the informant to do and by what date I expect him to have completed the work. It is important to limit the time an informant has to work for you. If you give him six months to get you information that leads to successful arrests, guess what? He'll take six months to get that information to you. On a simple under-the-influence or possession case, I give the informant no more than one month to fulfill the expectations I set in the contract. Remember, dopers are not the most motivated and successful people in the world. If they were, they probably wouldn't be using drugs and wouldn't have been caught. Set your expectations and keep them simple. You set them and yourself up for success with small achievable goals.

The contract my department uses begins with an information sheet that lists all of the necessary information pertinent to being able to identify the suspect and find him later. It also has a space for a photograph and rapsheet. Again, I cannot emphasize the importance of pulling the suspect's rapsheet and learning as much about him as possible before releasing him as a signed informant. Before you start to use that informant and most certainly before you attempt a controlled drug buy, you need to have your supervisor approve their employment.

## RELEASING THE INFORMANT

When you have made an on-sight arrest and completed your investigation and interview, you should know if the suspect is going to be a candidate to sign as an informant. And, if you have just signed up a person as a contractual informant, you must decide what to do with the arrest you just made. If it was an on-sight drug-related arrest and your supervisor approves of you doing so, let the person walk. Release him from your office or wherever you conducted your interview and write your report just like you would have if you took the person to jail and booked him. End your report with a sentence similar to "This investigation is ongoing" and don't submit it for a complaint. If you write that in an under-the-influence report, your boss should know you signed that person up as a confidential informant. Before you do release someone, make sure your supervisor understands what you are trying to do and get his permission first. You should have already discussed it with him so you have no questions or concerns about developing an informant at three o'clock in the morning while your boss is at home asleep. That is not the time to call him and ask for permission.

After I have decided a person is a candidate to be a confidential informant and I have written a contract that he has signed, I get as much information about drug houses and dealers and crime in general as I can before I let him leave. Once I have exhausted everything I can think of at the office, I have the informant lay down in the back seat of my patrol car and I drive around town and have him show me every house he knows that is selling dope and from whom he has purchased dope in the past. If I have a partner, I have him ride with us. I drive the informant around for a couple of reasons.

One, I thoroughly expect him to disappear and not work for me once I release him. I want to get as much information from him as I can before I let him walk. That way, if he disappears, my efforts weren't in vain. I still learned about a couple of new drug houses and I can get a warrant for his arrest and later find him for the offenses he committed that caused him to sign up as an informant in the first place. I'm not giving my arrest away; I'm just not getting it immediately. Second, I like the informant to physically show me the houses where he thinks he can buy drugs. If he actually does work and I end up conducting a controlled drug buy, I want firsthand intelligence about a drug house. I want the informant to point to the house as we are driving by and tell me everything he knows about the dealer, what he sells, how much, and to whom he sells. Again, if the informant flakes on me, I have still gained intelligence I can use later.

I always invite my partner to come with me during this first contact with the informant so one of us can drive and the other can take notes. If one is available, I have my partner sit in the interview with us and witness the contract. I never meet with my informant alone. I want him to get comfortable working with me and a partner. When I am working street-level dope and I actually have a partner, I include him on everything I learn and do. It makes my partners feels like they are part of a team and it helps build rapport and *esprit de corps* amongst us. And, working as a team is just safer. If I am working alone, I do everything the same. When I am driving around with an informant in the back of my car alone, I telephone dispatch and let them know what I am doing. After the initial arrest, I never meet with my informant when I am alone.

## MEETING INFORMANTS

After I have signed up an informant, I usually stay in contact with him by phone. Nearly all of the intelligence I need I can get from the informant by telephone. When I do meet with him, it is usually for the purpose of making a controlled drug buy and not just getting information. The more you meet with an informant in a marked patrol car, the more risk you take in "burning" your informant or having their confidentiality lost. If I do meet with an informant, I always take another deputy with me. Never meet with your informants alone, especially if you are male and your informant is female. I don't think much explanation is needed here. Avoid false allegations or problems when using female informants and always take someone with you when you meet with them. Always.

# ROAD BURNS

For the most part, a classical "road burn" is a stop you make after an informant has spoken with the dealer and agreed to meet him at a predetermined location for the purposes of buying drugs. Let's say your informant calls a dealer at your request and tells him he wants to buy an "eight ball." The informant might tell the dealer he doesn't have a car and ask him to meet in the Kmart parking lot in an hour. You know where the dealer is and which direction he will travel to get to the Kmart. You have no intention of purchasing the dope and your informant isn't at the Kmart; he should be with you. You know what the dealer is driving. Therefore, set yourself or your partner up somewhere between the dealer's location and the Kmart parking lot. You wait for the dealer to pass and when you see him, follow him and stop him for a vehicle code violation. In essence, you are making a "wall stop." You develop independent probable cause to arrest the driver or search him and his vehicle to get the "eight ball" you know he has because you ordered it through your informant. This is called a "road burn" and can be a useful tool while working a confidential informant.

"Road burns" are difficult to do alone and I almost always attempt them when I have a partner or two working with me. Sometimes, I will attempt a "road burn" the same night I arrest and sign up a confidential informant. I do this after I have driven around town with him and before I release him for the night. I like to do this then because the informant is with me and I can control the telephone call made to the dealer. I will keep the informant with me and have my partner make the stop on the dealer's car. I keep the informant laying down in my backseat if I drive to the stop and help my partner there. This is one type of "road burn."

I transferred to a small town in the western outskirts of my county that was predominantly an oilfield community. There were roughnecks and rig hands scattered amongst a lot of migrant farm workers. And there was a ton of dope in this little town. Some of the deputies assigned to the substation were new and some of them wanted to learn. I started to help one of my new partners develop his first confidential informant. About a week after he found his first C.I., the informant called him and told him a dealer was coming into town at around midnight bringing an ounce of meth with her. This dealer was female and we knew her from prior drug investigations. The informant told us what car she was driving and so we waited. There were only two main roads into town and he watched one and I took the other.

It was a Friday night and the calls for service started coming. Our other partner was running all over town and we were taking turns watching the roads and shagging calls. As I was leaving a call, I heard my partner make a traffic stop on the dealer's Mustang. I rolled up to back him and we contacted the driver. She wasn't on parole or probation and she had a valid driver's license. We did a drug evaluation on her, as she was still sitting in the driver's seat, and she was high. We arrested her for driving under-the-influence and we searched her car and purse. We found the ounce of meth in her purse. She had nothing else on her or in her car indicative of drug sales. So, after we towed her car and got her booked, we wrote a search warrant for her house looking for more dope and evidence that would help us build a better sales case. While she was out on bond, we conducted a controlled drug buy from her using the same informant who helped us set up the "road burn." She was later convicted of transportation for sales and sent to prison.

Although they sometimes aren't successful and they can be difficult to do while working patrol and responding to routine calls for service, "road burns" are potentially very effective tools and they are another means you can use to work your informants and get some quality arrests. If two out of ten "road burns" are successful, you are doing great. When you start to work a lot of street-level dope, you'll learn that finding dope is sometimes difficult even on those times when you have solid intelligence about the dope's location. Dope is an expendable item. It doesn't last long once it is manufactured and sold. The information lifespan pertaining to it can be only a few hours and sometimes less. If you strike out a few times when trying to set something up, don't get frustrated. It is part of the game. We as cops must get used to the fact that we are going to win a few and lose a bunch. This is what we have in common with defense attorneys. That's the game. But, if we stay with it, our victories will be huge.

# chapter seven
# The Controlled Buy

## "CONTROLLED"

If your department practices the use of confidential informants and controlled drug buys, you have a very powerful weapon available to you. You control the who, where, what, when, why, and how of the buy and you do this so you can later document the buy and use it as information in your probable cause to make an arrest or write a search warrant. Without controlled buys as a tool, you have to invest a lot more time and effort watching a drug house and making stops leaving that house before you can develop enough probable cause to write a search warrant. With most judges, a controlled buy gives you all the probable cause you need to convince them a particular person or house is involved in drug sales.

Throughout most of my career, I worked for supervisors who were proponents of the controlled buy and they supported me in my efforts to work confidential informants and make controlled drug buys. The times I worked for supportive sergeants were the most effective times I had in my career working street-level dope. I once worked for a sergeant who didn't feel comfortable allowing his deputies to make controlled buys on their own and when we signed up a confidential informant and wanted to make buys, he referred our informants over to our narcotics task force so they could use them. Not surprisingly, our number of arrests and our effectiveness was much less that it could have been. We didn't like giving our hard earned information over to someone else so they could potentially make a significant arrest. Although we didn't work dope for department recognition, we had our pride and didn't want to let someone else take credit for our hard work.

If you have an informant and are ready to use him to make a controlled buy, let your boss know. If your supervisor has never been involved in a controlled buy, show him your department's policy (if you have one) and tell him your plans on how the buy should go and what you plan on doing. This is the time for you to become a salesman and convince your boss it's a good idea and give him all of the benefits of successful buys. Tell him how you can use the information from the buy to write a search warrant for the house. Tell him how a press release about the execution of the search warrant not only makes his unit look good, it makes the department look good. When the public reads how deputies are aggressively pursuing drug dealers to help rid their neighborhoods of crime, it paints a positive picture of law enforcement. We all know how much bad press we receive. A controlled buy leading to a search warrant is one way we can create some positive press.

I was assigned to new substation a few years ago. I started making several possession arrests and I was gathering tons of information about drug dealers. It was just a matter of time before I found a good candidate to sign up as a confidential informant. Before it happened, I asked my sergeant what he thought about using informants and making controlled buys. He had never done a controlled buy and once I described it to him and showed him our department's policy, he thought it was a wonderful idea. Within a few days of talking with my sergeant, I arrested a guy for possession and signed him up as a contractual informant. About a week later, I was ready to make controlled buys with him. My sergeant got the funds needed and a cold car. Then, he and I drove to meet the informant one night on the outskirts of town. My sergeant completed the supervisor's interview with the informant and afterward we made a successful controlled buy of methamphetamine.

I wrote a search warrant for the house and person from whom we purchased the meth and a few days later we executed the search warrant. When we hit the house, the dealer wasn't there. We did get some dope however, and we answered the phone while we were at the house. We invited everyone who called to come over and by the end of the day, we had arrested nine people. Everyone in town heard what we were doing and later the local press covered our search warrant. We were on the front page of the local newspaper and our dispatch was flooded with phone calls from people praising us for "shutting down" a known drug house in their neighborhood. That year we made over twenty controlled buys and wrote as many search warrants all while working as uniformed patrolmen in a small substation.

## BEFORE, DURING, AND AFTER

What makes a controlled buy "controlled" are the steps you take before, during, and after the buy to make certain your informant purchases drugs from a specific person in a legal manner you can describe in your report. Much of the buy's success depends on how you present it to the informant and how you have managed your informant leading up to the buy. Most people are uncomfortable working with the cops and they are afraid their friends and the dealers will know what they are doing. Criminals are all afraid of being categorized as a "snitch" or a "rat." They have good reason for concern. There have been homicides resulting from botched drug deals and there have been informants killed because of what they did for and told the police. You can thwart off most of these concerns early when you sign up an informant by describing how the controlled buy actually works. This is how I describe the controlled buy to a potential informant.

*Here's how it works. Once I sign you up, nobody but my partner and my boss will know you are working for me. I won't drop by your house in a marked patrol car and I won't be telling everyone I arrest who you are. That would be stupid and I won't do it. The only way someone will know you are an informant is if you tell them. And that's on you. I will call you on the phone and if someone other than you answers, I won't tell them "This is deputy so and so …" I'll give them my first name and ask for you by your first name. I use my own personal cell phone so it doesn't come up "Sheriff's Office."*

*When we are going to do a controlled buy, I'll meet you somewhere* in an unmarked car. Usually it is like a red Suburban or green Durango. We'll pick a spot outside of town in the hills somewhere and I'll meet you there with my partner. I'll search you and make sure you have nothing on you. I normally take everything you have so it is easier for me to search you after the buy. Once I have searched you and make sure you have no dope on you, I'll give you a twenty or forty and then we'll drive to the house. I won't drive right up to the house. I'll park down the block or somewhere away where I can watch you walk up to the house and watch you leave. I'll pick a spot where I can keep you in sight at all times. I usually have binoculars and watch you with those.

Once you make the purchase, you will leave the house and walk back to my car. You'll give me the dope and then I'll drive you to another isolated spot and I'll search you again for any other dope or contraband. Then, I'll drive us to another house and we'll do it again. If we can, we'll make two or three buys just like the first. Once we're done, I'll drive you back to your car or wherever you want and leave. Then, I'll write a search warrant for the house and a few days later, we'll take them down. I'm not going to go rushing in and arrest the guy right after you leave. That would burn you and I'm not going to do that.

When I write my reports you'll be listed as "X." I will never list your name in a report and if the defense attorney demands to know who you are, there are rules that allow me to keep your name confidential. If for some bizarre reason we have to disclose your name to make the case, I'll have the DA drop the charges. No amount of dope is worth your safety and I won't let your identity be known just to make a case.

After I tell this to the potential informants, I let them ask any questions and I answer them truthfully. Usually, their biggest concern is having their identity released and it becoming know they are working for the cops. If you sell yourself and describe the controlled buys to them and what you expect them to do, it will help ease their minds about what controlled buys are about. Remember to tell them they're working off a case. It's a job and sometimes jobs are not easy. But, if they want to avoid jail or having a criminal record, this is their only way out.

Before the controlled buy, I talk to the informant on the phone several times and get as much information as I can about the dealers he can buy from. I get their names, addresses, vehicle information, friends and associates, and any intelligence the informant can provide. Then,

I conduct surveillance on the house to corroborate the informant. If what he tells me seems accurate, then I set up a time to meet him and make the controlled buys. If I have a "cold car" or an unmarked county vehicle that doesn't have an "E" plate, I make arrangements to use it. Of course, I have a partner with me and I get permission from my supervisor beforehand. I'll discuss using a marked patrol car as a last resort later in this chapter.

Then, I call the informant and have him meet us at a secluded location. Once I meet the informant, I search him and seize everything from him. I have him leave his car there. If he doesn't have a car, I make arrangements to pick him up somewhere he feels comfortable. I have driven a "cold car" to an informant's house before to pick him up for controlled buys. I let the informant decide where he is comfortable meeting. A convenient store or gas station is a common place where I have picked up my informants for controlled buys. If he has a car, have him meet you somewhere.

Once he is searched, we leave the meeting spot and set up the buy. I ask my informant how he usually buys. If he telephones the dealer ahead of time, then we do that. If he can drop in unannounced, then we do that. Whatever is normal and doesn't raise suspicion is how you want to have your informant make the controlled buy. It should be natural and eventless. These types of buys will help you avoid the need of using a Hobb's Order in your search warrant. I'll explain the Hobb's Order in more detail in the chapter on search warrants.

Once the informant has done whatever he needed to do to prepare the dealer for his arrival, we drive to the house. I park far enough away that the informant can walk to the dealer's house. If the dealer is standing outside waiting for him, I might drive closer if the C.I. is comfortable. I do this to not raise any suspicions. If the dealer sees me park way down the street and then the informant walks up to him, he's going to want to know who is in the car with him and why he parked so far away. If it isn't normal, then it is suspicious. I give the informant money and watch him walk to the dealer's house. If he goes inside, I watch to see if anyone else enters. It is important to keep your informant visible and actually watch him walk from your vehicle to the dealer's house. This is part of what makes the buy "controlled." I watch the informant leave the house and try to never lose sight of him.

Once the informant gets back into the car, I take the dope from him and drive to another isolated location. There, I search him again to ensure he has only the dope he just purchased with him. I also check to make sure he doesn't have my money. Immediately after the buy, I ask the informant to tell me how much dope the dealer had, how much he saw, where the dealer kept the dope, and if he went somewhere to retrieve it, I ask him where he went. If it was another room, I ask which room. I get as much intelligence as I can when it is fresh in the informant's mind. After all, in a few days I will likely be searching the house for dope and I want to make my job during that search as easy as possible. If there are other houses we planned on buying from, we drive there and do it again. I repeat the process for each house. I put the dope from each buy in separate bags so they don't get mixed up and I don't get confused. After the buys, I return to the office, book the dope, and write my reports.

## DOCUMENTING THE BUY

Controlled buy reports are very short and simple. They include the evidence and a paragraph or two detailing the buy. I pull one case number per buy and I list which partner was with me during the buy. When I refer to the informant, I list him as "X." I am careful to avoid the use of pronouns identifying my informant's gender. I list the circumstances surrounding the buy and if I can, I list the dealer and his address. If I don't have the dealer identified, I list him however the informant knows him. If the dealer at the time of the buy is known only as "Freddy," then I list him like that. The controlled buy report is only for the department's use and to detail the evidence and chain of evidence since a controlled substance was purchased. Otherwise, it will not be used for any purposes later. Of course, what happened during the controlled buy will be used as part of the probable cause for the search warrant later. You don't need to use the case number though.

## COLD CAR vs. PATROL CAR

Using a "cold car" during controlled buys is one of the few times I work street-level dope when I am not in a marked patrol car or in uniform. Obviously, it is always better to do controlled buys in plain clothes and driving an unmarked vehicle. I have, however, done one controlled buy from a marked patrol car in full uniform. There are times when an informant wants to work for you immediately. Sometimes, that is a good time to use him. If you get your supervisor to trust you and gain his confidence, he might just give you buy money and the discretion to make controlled buys on your own. That doesn't usually happen and I've only had a couple of sergeants who gave me that trust. If you find yourself in a situation where you want to use an informant and make a controlled buy while you are in uniform and you don't have a "cold car" available to use, you do the controlled buy the same as you would normally. The difference is where you park. If you are in a marked patrol car, your surveillance spot might be the best location to drop off the informant and watch him make the buy. All you have to do is be a little more creative and think "outside the box" a little bit more. While you are driving around with your informant, have him lay across the back seat. If your informant is comfortable making the buy with you in uniform and from your patrol car, do it. The prep, surveillance during the buy, the search afterward, and the report documenting the buy are otherwise the same. And, remember to have a partner with you.

Don't rule out the possibility of making controlled buys just because you don't have a "cold car" designated specifically for that purpose. You might have a citizen volunteer car or a four wheel drive assigned to your station. If something comes up and you want to try a buy, grab one of those cars. If you don't have plain clothes, take off your uniform shirt and do the buy in your t-shirt. I have done buys in my t-shirt while wearing my green wool uniform pants and boots. Have your informant bring you a couple of baseball hats or over-shirts if you don't have time to go home and change. My motto is *Sempre Gumby* or "always flexible." Be able to adapt to the situation and improvise. Sometimes, working street-level dope isn't always black and white. There are times you've got to create the shades of gray if you want to make things happen.

## CAVEAT

I recall one afternoon doing probation and parole searches as part of a small task force. It was a planned operation my substation conducted. I wasn't the coordinator of the sweep; I was just a participant. Later in the afternoon after the searches were over, my sergeant came back to the office with a guy he had arrested for possession of a crank pipe. The guy was a bit loony and he was high as a kite. To keep from going to jail, he sang like a canary for my sergeant and told him he could buy dope for him. My sergeant was excited about controlled buys after doing his first one with me a few weeks before. He wanted me and another deputy to take the guy and go buy some dope that evening.

I had read our policy on using informants and knew it was a bad idea to use an informant who was still under-the-influence. My partner and I both warned the sergeant and tried to talk him into waiting and using this guy to make buys another time after he was sober. Well, my boss was very pro-active and wanted to get something going and do the buys right then. I respected him for his enthusiasm and support. My partner and I were both experienced in doing controlled buys and we thought to ourselves, "What could go wrong?"

Well, we loaded our new found tweaker friend in our under cover car that happened to be an allied agency's Toyota Celica and off we went. Our informant was so spun he wouldn't shut up. We gave him twenty dollars for the first buy and before we even got to the house, he lost it. We had to stop and search the car for our buy money! The tweaker had crunched the twenty inside some garbage left in the car. Neither one of us trusted this guy, so we sent him into the first house with a cell phone so we could keep in contact with him. At our first house, the guy disappeared for about thirty minutes. My partner called him and asked him, "What the hell! Are you blowing a bowl in there or what? Let's go!" We had to threaten to come in and arrest the guy to get him to come outside. Well, he returned with some dope but we both thought he probably used a quarter of it before he left. On and on we went through the night with one folly after another. We eventually made a few successful buys, but we learned why our policy advised against using informants when they are high. We passed this information along to our sergeant and we all had a pretty good laugh. And, we never had that problem again.

If you schedule a time to meet your informant and he shows up high, do not use him. In fact, I recommend you arrest him for being under-the-influence. The last thing you want when conducting a controlled buy is to have your informant spun on dope and taking your money into a dope house. Remember, tweakers are unpredictable and their behavior is paranoid and they can become volatile. Tell your informants when they sign the contract that if they meet you and they're high, you are going to arrest them. The idea for them being informants in the first place is to work off a case and try to stay clean. If they can't stay sober long enough to meet you at a scheduled time for controlled buys, they aren't worthy of your favor. Arrest them and cancel their contract.

Using informants and making controlled drug buys is the epitome of combining everything you have learned working street-level dope. Being able to successfully work an informant to write and execute a search warrant to find dope and make an arrest can be a remarkable skill that will help you advance your abilities and sometimes your career. Remember, you can have a successful controlled drug buy and still strike out when searching for dope in a house. Expect to find dope in about one out of five search warrants and you won't be disappointed. If your successes are greater than that, terrific! Being able to work informants and conduct controlled drug buys doesn't guarantee your success. It does, however, turn that pendulum of *Luck vs. Skill* in your favor. And, that is your goal.

# Chapter Eight
# Language And Psychology

## COLLOQUIAL LANGUAGE

I received a citizen complaint years ago alleging I used profanity with the public. My department, like many, has a written policy that specifically states no employees shall use profanity while dealing with the public. Normally, I don't cuss much when handling my calls and doing routine police work. One Halloween, I was working patrol and I received several complaints about juveniles stealing candy from trick-or-treaters and causing problems in a nicer residential neighborhood. I didn't have a reported victim; the complainants only wanted a law enforcement presence in the area as a deterrent.

I directed my patrol in the area and soon, I found three juveniles, not wearing Halloween costumes, who started running from me when I turned the corner. I caught the kids, who were around fourteen or fifteen years old, and knew they were my hood rats causing the problems. None of them lived in the neighborhood and although they were not yet certified gang members, it was apparent they were on the path to some initiation.

All three had attitudes and when I snatched them up and tossed them in the back of my car, I didn't get any compliance or respect. I spoke with them professionally and courteously. That, however, didn't work. My tone quickly changed and I read them the riot act. When they realized I was upset about them stealing candy from little kids and told them I would not allow it (in not so many words,) I got their undivided attention and their carefree, arrogant attitudes, disappeared. Suddenly, answers like, "Yes, sir" and "No, sir" became part of their juvenile vocabulary.

Well, I didn't arrest them and I drove them home and released them to their parents with a warning. The following Monday, I received a complaint alleging I used profanity and threatened to kill the kids, drag their bodies into the desert, and bury them. Then, I would make the parents come and dig up their bodies. Wow! I said all of that? You know how complaints go. Well, it didn't end there. Since I was accused of violating a department policy, a full internal affairs investigation was conducted and a few months later, I found myself sitting with the internal affairs sergeant, in a little office, with his tape recorder on the desk.

He read the allegations and policy violation to me and asked me what happened. With a laugh, I told him I didn't say what they said I did. However, I told the sergeant that if I had thought of it at the time, I would have! I explained colloquial language and when it is appropriate and even more effective than Standard English. The sergeant knew what colloquial meant, but he wanted me to explain it to him, "On the record." So, I told him it was informal language commonly used amongst a certain group of people. I told him it was "slang."

I understood how and when to use certain slang terms and vocabulary, which sometimes included profanity, when trying to communicate effectively with certain groups of people. I told him, for instance, if I stopped a doper on the street, I wasn't going to say to him, "Good evening sir. May I inquire as to when you use last ingested methamphetamine?" No. I would probably speak his language and ask him, "Dude, what the fuck you are doing sneaking around in the dark like this? Did you use some shit today?" And I continued to explain myself and I told him I knew when to select certain language to use and when to use it effectively. I told him I wouldn't talk to a doctor or a rape victim like I would a parolee at large I just found hiding under a house.

So, in regards to the complaint, I detailed the events surrounding Halloween night and what I saw and how the juveniles were speaking to me. I told the sergeant professional and polite language was ineffective in that circumstance, because I tried. So, I selected more harsh vocabulary, including profanity, to resolve the problem and make an impact. A couple of weeks later, I received the disposition letter in the mail and learned the internal affairs review board exonerated me on the policy violation of using profanity with the public. In short, they determined my language was "okay" given the circumstances.

When dealing with drug addicts or any criminal for that matter, you must use language appropriate to their level of understanding. You have to lower yourself, verbally, to their level sometimes to be able to understand them and have them understand you. Let's face it; we don't normally deal with college educated people. I'm not saying college educated people don't break the law, because we all know some do. But mostly, college educated, professional, scholastic people aren't walking in the alley at three o'clock in the morning looking for their next fix.

You can learn doper language through experience and by simply asking. When I arrest a semi cooperative addict and I am interviewing him, I ask him about drugs. After all, he's the expert. I ask what words he uses to describe his dope. I ask him how often he uses or maybe why he slams instead of smoking it. I want to know how much he spends buying drugs and where he buys. If he doesn't have a job, I ask him where he gets money for dope. Sometimes, he'll tell you he's a burglar and then you can ask him about burglaries. I ask him when he started using and why. I ask him to describe to me what it feels like getting high. If I don't know something, I ask. If I don't know how to "blow a bowl" or make a crank pipe, I ask him how he makes his. If I get a really cooperative doper who I might later sign up as a contractual informant, I ask even more personal questions. I ask him where he hides his dope to avoid being arrested. I'll ask him if he ever "keisters" his dope and when. I've asked dopers to tell me, "If you were me, how would you clean up this town?" Ask a doper this and you will probably get a damn good answer. They might tell you to arrest "so and so" because he is the biggest dealer in town.

# RAPPORT BUILDING

When you begin to arrest numerous drug addicts, you will often arrest the same person two, three, or more times. I arrested a doper five times once in a year. To be effective in working street-level dope, you must learn to establish a good rapport with as many crooks as possible. Eventually, you will have a reputation on the street. How you conduct your dealings with those you arrest will determine the reputation you develop in the drug community. When you arrest a drug addict, don't treat him like a piece of dirt. Sometimes, as life turns, a former booking number you arrested may be your only ally.

I was working a graveyard shift one night in a very rural desert town. My nearest back-up was a bordering county deputy and I could expect his emergency response time to be anywhere between thirty minutes to an hour. I was sent to the local American Legion Bar, which sadly, didn't have a bunch of veterans drinking there, but a gang of local tweakers who were either on probation or parole. There was a reported large fight in the parking lot and some of the players were armed with knives. When I arrived, three or four were still fighting. That didn't particularly concern me much. I learned long ago to let them tire themselves out and then swoop in and handle business. As the fight ended, I tried to separate the group and settle things down. After I ran a records check on the bunch, I learned one was a parolee at large who was listed as "armed and dangerous."

I told the parolee to turn around and put his hands behind his back. He challenged me to fight and told me he wasn't going back to jail. A few of his friends sided with him and told me I was not going to arrest him. I soon found myself very outnumbered, but I was stubborn and I told the guy he could either go with me to jail or the county morgue in a body bag. I could see him thinking and before he answered me, I saw someone walking through the crowd behind me. I turned to face an old booking number I had arrested for felony drug charges some time ago. This guy walked up and stood next to me.

He told the parolee he wasn't going to do anything and he'd personally break his legs if he didn't listen to me. Soon, the rest of the crowd sided with us and I was able to arrest the parolee without a fight. Once the guy was handcuffed and seated in the back of my car, I shook hands with my former booking number and we "bumped fists."

I vaguely remembered arresting him for drug possession and he told me that when I arrested him, I treated him with respect and he always remembered me. He told me, "I've got no hard feelings. You were just doing your job." He said he wished there were more cops like me then he disappeared into the crowd and back to his friends. That was quite a memorable event and lesson I will never forget.

## PARENT – TEENAGER RELATIONSHIP

The best way to deal with the drug offender, and sometimes all criminals, is to create a parent/teenager relationship. We all remember being teenagers. We weren't in charge, but our parents didn't talk to us like little kids either. They would share with us some of the household decisions and get our input. But, ultimately, the final decision was theirs and we knew and respected this. We were more likely to get along with our parents when they treated us equally instead of looking down at us like we were just stupid kids who didn't know anything. If they treated us well, we weren't as likely to rebel when they did something or told us to do something we didn't like.

The cops are the parents. We enforce the laws and the crooks are the teenagers who must obey the laws. We treat teenagers like responsible adults until they make us treat them like little kids. They choose how the meeting will go and how we will treat them. Mostly, when you talk to people showing them decency and respect, they will return that respect. Sometimes, dopers are under-the-influence of drugs and how they act when they are high is not the same as they act when they are sober. Remember this. They're just like drunks. And, sometimes you can't deal rationally with a drunk. So, if they don't behave like you expect them to, don't get angry. If they're acting like punks, be as polite as you can and do your job.

## PSYCHOLOGY

Being able to get people to do what you want them to do sometimes involves more psychology than you'd think. When you are taking the freedom away from someone and becoming responsible for their every need, you can't do it without using a degree of psychology on them. Cops have to be amateur psychologists to know how to speak to people to get them to comply. Words are used more in police work than physical force. When you are working street-level dope, your ability to analyze the personality types of dopers enables you to get the information from them you need to make your case.

Sometimes, you'll find the angry doper who blames his drug usage on everyone but himself. If he's angry, fine. Understand his anger and empathize with him. If he started using because his wife left him, talk about an experience you've had with infidelity. We all know someone who has been through a divorce or separation as a result of a cheating spouse. Some of us have experienced this ourselves. Find some common ground and focus on that. Tell him you understand and don't blame him at all. If you have to, allow him to woman bash and agree with him. You'll know pretty soon if this tactic is going to work. If it doesn't, then just maintain your professionalism and do your job. Finish your paperwork, get the guy booked, and move on.

Most dopers don't want to be addicts and if you ask them, they'll probably admit to having a drug problem. These are great statements and I always include them in my reports. I would list in my report, "I asked him if he thought he had a drug problem." He replied, "I know I do." I asked him, "Do you think you need help?" And he said, "Yes, I do." These are admissions and even if it doesn't apply to evidence pertaining to the arrest, it's still useful. If you can get someone to admit to being a drug addict and needing help, you can take on the role of the therapist and ask him how you can help. You are using psychology. It isn't rocket science. It's common sense.

If you have worked patrol for more than three days, you know your ability to talk to people is key whether you are handling calls for service or hunting warrant suspects. How you present yourself, the tone you use, the language you use, your ability to be a brother, a doctor, a financial advisor, a marriage counselor, a father, a son, a mother, a school teacher, a priest, a husband, a psychologist, and every other role possible, determines whether you succeed or fail. When working street-level dope, you continue to play those roles. Your interpersonal communication skills and your ability to make psychology work for you can help you become a good street-level dope cop. Your inability to do these things helps you become one of those useless liabilities I spoke about earlier. The choice is yours.

# chapter nine
# Documentation

## STYLE

Personal writing styles are as unique as fingerprints; nobody writes the same. Your education level and experience influences how you write. This same experience determines how effectively you do write. It seems, despite the volume of reports officers write throughout their careers, those who never liked writing and who weren't very good at it in the first place, never seem to get any better. For some reason, cops think they know English and can already write. So, they make no effort to improve. Some officers can write decent, intelligible reports; but most can't. Since I believe report writing skills are sometimes more important than the arrest and investigation, I will offer some suggestions to help you write better reports.

## HANDWRITING

My dad was a police detective and learned as a young patrolman to write in block letters. He was very particular about his printing and it was very neat. I always liked the way my dad wrote and when I was in the fourth grade, he taught me to write in block letters. My teachers didn't like this style, because they were still teaching us about proper nouns like "Indian," and when I wrote in block letters they couldn't grade my ability to know these nouns. But, they got used to my new writing style when I told them my dad was a cop and wanted me to write this way. My printing before was average. When I started copying my dad's handwriting, the neatness and quality of my work improved ten fold and my teachers acknowledged this.

I learned there was a psychological connection between how neat my work looked and the quality it contained. When I started taking the time to write neat homework assignments, I actually started learning more, I did my homework correctly, and my grades improved. I enjoyed my new found success so much I even looked forward to writing assignments. My dad saw the improvement and when I was in high school and could understand, he told me about writing police reports.

He told me that as a detective, he read reports from officers he never met. He judged their ability as cops based on their reports. If he saw a report face sheet printed neatly with no spelling or grammar errors, he expected the content of the report to be good. On the contrary, if he read a report with poor penmanship and it looked like the officer scribbled the report in haste, he expected there to be all sorts of problems with the arrest and investigation. He told me that more often than not, neatly printed reports were better than ones sloppy in appearance. He said he knew district attorneys who would only file cases if the report appeared neat and in order. If the officer's handwriting was messy, the DA figured the case was probably weak. He said one attorney actually admitted to him that if the report isn't written neatly and prepared with care, he doesn't even read it.

By my senior year in high school, I had already completed the necessary classes to graduate. I knew I was going in the Army after I graduated and not college, so I didn't take college preparatory classes and other academic types of classes. No, I took a couple of PE classes, a double lunch, library, etc. Well, you get the picture. My girlfriend at the time was in an English class, so I signed up for it just to spend time with her. I was a true scholar and a gentleman! Since the class didn't effect whether or not I graduated, I decided to experiment and test the lesson my dad taught me about penmanship.

Every Friday, the English teacher gave a spelling and definition test.

She assigned twenty-five words on Monday and on Friday she walked up and down the rows of desks and dictated the words. We had to spell the words correctly and then write their definitions. Had she chosen words we were likely use again in our lifetimes, it would have been a great learning tool. Instead, she chose a bunch of stupid words I had never heard up to that point. In fact, I still haven't heard or used those words in my life!

On one particular test, I didn't study and I knew I was going to get an "F." But, instead of turning in a blank piece of paper, I decided to experiment and take the test. I knew how to spell and I was certain I could spell the words correctly. So, I marked my paper one through twenty-five and left a couple of spaces between each line to write the definitions. I printed the words like it was a job application and I took my time. There wasn't a blemish or stray mark on the paper. I made certain all of the letters were the same height and width and I watched carefully to lean them all to the right symmetrically.

Once I had written the words, I made up outrageous definitions off the top of my head and I filled up the entire page with a bunch of nonsense. I used humor of course and avoided profanity. It was really great fun. Aesthetically, it looked super! I used the entire hour allocated for the test and nonchalantly handed my paper in with the rest of the students. I didn't tell anyone what I did. I just did it. Monday she handed the spelling tests back to us and I expected to see a red "F" written in the top right. To my surprise, I saw a big "A+" written on the right highlighted with a circle. Holy cow! The teacher didn't even read the definitions. She looked at how the paper appeared and must have thought that if I took the time to print as neatly as I did, I certainly knew all of the definitions. Wow! That was an amazing lesson I learned about how people are judged based on how they write.

From that day forward, I took even more time and effort to write neatly. I used that skill throughout my years in the Army and carried it over into my career in law enforcement. When I first started working patrol, we handwrote our face sheets and shorter reports. I found the DA was filing on nearly every report I submitted. And, by virtue of working patrol and writing reports based on department policy and state law, I wrote reports on some things that were barely crimes. Not only should I have not written some of the reports, the DA most certainly shouldn't have been filing them. One day while I was sitting in court on a case that should have been dismissed, I asked the DA why he didn't reject the case for insufficient evidence.

He was amazed at my question and he said, "You took so much time to write your report neatly, I figured it was a good case and you wanted it to go to trial." I chuckled and told him I didn't take any time to write that report or do any investigation. I told him I always wrote like that. After that day, he started to actually read my reports and then started filing the ones he should and dismissing the others. I was pleased he was filing my cases, but tired of spending my days off in court on stupid cases filed from reports I wrote only because I had to.

## SPELLING, PUNCTUATION, AND GRAMMAR

The absence of punctuation, the presence of spelling errors, or too much punctuation is an obvious sign to an attorney or knowledgeable reader that you don't know English. I could spend three chapters giving basic English lessons, but instead I'm going to refer you to "The Little Brown Handbook." If you don't know when to use a comma or what punctuation is appropriate, you need to do some research. If you aren't sure how to spell a word, look it up in a dictionary or use a different word you know how to spell. Nothing makes you look worse to your supervisors and attorneys than misspelled words throughout your report. It tells them you either don't know how to spell or you don't care enough to proofread. Both of theses scenarios are bad and you want to avoid them.

## PROOFREAD

When I have free time, I get old reports I have written and I re-read them looking for mistakes. Although I take great pride in my reports and I proofread usually two or three times before I turn in a report for approval, I can still find one or two mistakes in my own reports. Imagine how many mistakes I would find if I didn't proofread at all! When I write a report, either by hand or by typing it myself, immediately after I have finished I read through it completely looking for punctuation and spelling errors. This is my once through proofread and normally I can catch obvious mistakes. If I have time, I set the report aside for a couple of hours and then read it again. During this read, I can sometimes find more errors. If you dictate your report you must be even more cautious of how your report reads before you submit it for approval. Naturally, we don't talk like we write and your report will sometimes read poorly. Clerks are a godsend to police officers, but not all of them are very good typists or English majors. Some will type in all of your mistakes and misused words and make your report look horrible. If you have the chance, proofread your dictations before they are submitted for a complaint.

For some reason, when you read through your report immediately after you have written it, you tend to read right through some of your mistakes. I suppose it is because you know what you want to say and little things like the incorrect use or "your" or "you're" don't catch your eye. When you proofread, you have to read your own work critically as if you didn't write it. You have to look at every word to make sure the correct "their" or "there" has been used. Look for possessive words and the proper use of apostrophes. Make sure there aren't any fragment sentences or proper nouns not capitalized. Again, if you don't know the rules and how to use punctuation, teach yourself. Research punctuation and grammar and make yourself an expert in English. After all, it is our national language.

## YOUR REPUTATION

I can't emphasize enough the importance of writing neat, grammatically correct, and accurate reports. Your reputation is at stake and in law enforcement today, your reputation sometimes is everything. Take pride in everything you do especially when your name is written at the bottom. Don't be a normal officer and write typical police reports; because they aren't good. Be the exception to the rule. Learn proper English and know when to use punctuation. Proofread your work two or three times before submitting it for approval. Be the officer who takes pride in his work and when attorneys get copies of your reports, be proud that they assume you must have done a good investigation and made a good arrest because of how neat your report was written. If your reports are crap, all the great police work in the world doesn't matter if the district attorney doesn't feel comfortable filing your arrests for a complaint. You owe it to yourself, your department, and the community to give one hundred percent and improve your weaknesses when it comes to report writing.

# chapter ten
# The Search Warrant

## THE MYSTIQUE

When I first started my career as a patrolman, I was sent to a desert community with a population of about 25,000. At the time, it seemed only rookies were being sent to the desert and the deputy with the most seniority there had no more than two years working the streets. We were a motivated group of youngsters and we arrested everything that walked or crawled. We were competitive and were all developing our skills as street-level dope cops. We conducted nightly parole and probation searches and every now and then, we found dope. We soon learned how to watch houses and make stops leaving suspected drug locations. We understood probable cause and discussed writing search warrants. However, none of us had ever done one and quite frankly, we were intimidated.

On our computer's desktop in the substation squad room was a search warrant template. Not surprising, the template was blank. But, it was there. We worked several cases and many times had enough probable cause to write search warrants. Instead of writing the search warrants, though, we used every trick and tool we could think of to avoid them. We worked really hard at avoiding them. We relied heavily on consent and probation search terms. We found "consent to search" forms in our filing cabinet and thought those were great! We had our suspects sign them like winning lottery tickets and we strolled around with consent forms like gods! If those options weren't available to us, we stretched the search incident to arrest to the max. We stretched it far at times and walked the line. I went through the first year of my career deathly afraid of the search warrant and until I met an injured child one night, I never wrote one.

One evening while I was working alone, I received a call of a possible child abuse situation at the local hospital. When I arrived, I learned I was soon going to be the lead investigator on a felony child abuse investigation. I met a two-year-old boy in the emergency room with a fractured leg. The child was screaming in pain and was frightened. Because of his age, he couldn't tell me what happened. The pain in his eyes and the comfort he felt when I held him told the story. Dad's statement of how the child broke the bone was absurd. He said the child must have "accidentally" rolled off the couch while he stepped into the other room for a moment. The couch was about a foot and a half off the floor. The fracture was so severe the doctor said the child would have had to jump off the roof to receive the injury. The x-rays showed the bone was a spiral fracture and dad's theory flew out the window. I knew immediately I needed help. Luckily, there was a newly promoted detective working as the night supervisor in a nearby substation. I called him and within hours, I was writing my first search warrant.

He helped me write a telephonic search warrant for dad's house. The search warrant was to gather evidence to try and find out what actually happened to the child. We needed to measure the height of the couch to disprove his story and we wanted to look for evidence that dad had become angry and violent. The detective knew the on duty judge personally and actually made the call himself. Although I wrote the probable cause declaration for the search warrant affidavit, he made the call and recorded it. I did get to watch and learn. He helped me from start to finish and by the time we secured dad's house and after processing it with our technical investigator, I learned the mystique about search warrants was self created. Oh, and I arrested dad for felony child abuse.

Once I completed my first search warrant with the help of a veteran officer, I learned that if you can write a probable cause declaration and complete an emergency protective order, you can write a search warrant. Once I cracked the code, I was amazed at how simple it was to write and serve a search warrant. I learned it was, by far, the most important investigative tool in a police officer's war bag. After I started writing dope search warrants, I realized that once you have your expertise clause written and have a copy of your search warrant saved on a disc, all you have to do is cut and paste and change the dates, addresses, and names. Understanding the search warrant and its components is simple. There are three parts to a search warrant beginning with the affidavit.

## AFFIDAVIT

The search warrant affidavit is the meat and potatoes of the search warrant. It is where you introduce to the judge the who, where, what, when, why, and how of your case. It includes your expertise or "hero clause" commonly referred to on dope search warrants. And, most importantly, it gives the probable cause for the search. An affidavit is a formal sworn statement, signed by the declarant, or affiant, that is present before a Magistrate. Basically, when you give a search warrant to a judge to be signed, he will have you raise your right hand and swear the information contained in the affidavit is the truth. He will then ask you to sign the affidavit. You swear in when you testify in court hearings and you do the same before the judge who will sign and authorize your search warrant.

Every department has search warrant templates. Some might appear different, but most contain the same information. Find a template your agency uses and keep a copy of it on a disc or flash drive. When you are ready to write your first search warrant, it should be nothing harder than filling in the blanks. If you work with someone who has already written a search warrant, make yourself a copy and all you'll have to do is cut and paste. I have compiled a bunch of search warrants over the years and have them saved to a folder on my computer at work. If I write a search warrant, I save it there. If someone else has written a search warrant for something I haven't, I keep a copy of theirs for the day when I need it for a specific reason. For example, you might need to get a Buccal DNA swab someday from a suspect and having a template specific for that evidence will save you time.

## EXPERTISE

Part of your affidavit includes your expertise. This is the area where you list your training and experience geared toward the specific evidence you are searching for. If you are writing a search warrant for methamphetamine, list your training specific to that drug. Once you have your expertise prepared, it doesn't change. If you attend another class or school, all you have to do is add that training to your expertise. For search warrants other than dope, your expertise might be much broader and less specific.

A couple of years ago, I was working a burglary case where the suspect left an Albertson's receipt at the scene. I went to the Albertson's store where the suspect made the purchase and learned he wrote a personal check. Albertson's had already sent the check to the bank and it was somewhere in transit. The store had the routing number to the check, but not a copy of it. Without the check, I wasn't able to learn who was on the account. I telephoned a local bank and learned the check routing number returned to another bank. I wrote a search warrant for the account holder and his information based off of the routing number. I had never written a search warrant for bank records before, so I telephoned a friend of mine who worked financial crimes in our detective division. He emailed me a copy of a search warrant he wrote recently for bank records and I cut and pasted my information onto his. The expertise he used for the search warrant was very basic and so was mine. However, it was sufficient for that search warrant and I have used that template three times on other investigations involving financial records.

Don't get caught up in the fact you are a new officer and have little experience or no expertise. If all you have is the basic academy training and a few months on patrol, list that experience. You don't need to write a Pulitzer Prize winning "hero clause" to qualify yourself as an expert. Remember, you are an expert because you do have a significant amount of training compared to John Q. Public. You have made a certain number of drug-related arrests. You have talked with known drug users and other officers about certain types of drugs. Just make certain you don't embellish or list schools and training you are scheduled to attend. If you haven't actually received the training or attended the school, leave it out of your expertise.

## PROBABLE CAUSE

We as law enforcement officers make our living using probable cause. District attorneys make theirs on reasonable doubt; which is a higher burden of proof than probable cause. We use probable cause everyday, on every call, and most certainly on every arrest we make. Your probable cause for a search warrant affidavit is no different. All you have to do is articulate in your probable cause why you want to search a certain person or location, what you want to search for, how you learned the stuff is there, where you want to search, and the judge will give you ten days to do it answering the question of "When?" Like I said before, if you can write a probable cause declaration and an emergency protective order, you can write a search warrant. I include the emergency protective order because you have to present it to a judge or via a telephone call to get the emergency protective order granted. Remember the first time you got an emergency protective order? I bet you were nervous and afraid the judge would call you stupid or something. Right? Well, once you did one, the rest were a piece of cake. Search warrants are no different. Once your first one is under your belt, you'll be able to scratch one out in no time.

## THE SEARCH WARRANT

The actual search warrant is just a copy of the portion of your affidavit granting the locations, vehicles, and persons to be searched. It is the second part of a search warrant. I cut and paste from my affidavit to the search warrant when I prepare one. The expertise and probable cause for the search contained within the affidavit is not in the actual search warrant. The reason is because you will give your suspect a copy of the search warrant and he doesn't need to know your expertise and probable cause. His attorney might request it later as discovery, but that's his problem, not yours. If you used an informant to develop your probable cause for the search warrant, sometimes the details would reveal your informant's identity. The suspect might know him based off of those facts. If this is the case, you can request a Hobb's Order to protect and seal a portion or all of the probable cause contained in the affidavit. I'll discuss the Hobb's Order in more detail later in this chapter.

When the judge signs the search warrant, he will give it back to you. You file a copy of it with the court. The judge will usually direct you to his clerk who will do this for you. Some judges will keep the original affidavit, but all will give you the original copy of the search warrant. Make two copies of the search warrant and one of the affidavits. When you serve the warrant, you will leave a copy of the search warrant either with the suspect or at his house. You will attach one copy of the search warrant and affidavit to your report after the search warrant and you will return the original search warrant to the judge with your receipt and search warrant return.

## THE SEARCH WARRANT RETURN

The search warrant return is the third part of the search warrant and is the last thing you will do once you have served the warrant. From the date and time the judge signs and authorizes the search warrant, you have ten days to complete the search warrant and the return. For every search warrant I have written and served, this is ample time. It is possible to file a request with the court to extend the time you have to file the search warrant return. I have never needed to do this, but you can if circumstances require you to hold it and exceed the normal ten day service period. The search warrant return consists of the original search warrant listing the date and time the search warrant was executed. It includes a copy of the receipt you give to the suspect itemizing everything seized pursuant to the search, and it includes a page entitle "Search Warrant Return." It is basically a packet you prepare and give to the judge. When you present it to him, he will swear you in again and you will sign the return in front of him. He too will sign the return and he will probably direct you to his clerk again to file it with the court.

## HOBB'S ORDER

A Hobb's Order allows you to request that a portion or all of your search warrant affidavit probable cause declaration be sealed by the Magistrate in order to protect your informant's identity. The Hobb's Orders I have used are an attachment that goes with the affidavit. When

I prepare a Hobb's Order, I cut and paste the section of the probable cause declaration I want to keep confidential. Usually, it is a portion of the probable cause specific enough in detail that if the suspect was able to read it, he would know who informed on him.

One night I was using an informant to make controlled buys. The informant knew of a guy who was selling dope, but he didn't know him personally. He called a female friend and arranged to meet her at her apartment. Then, she was going to call the dealer and have him come to her apartment to sell him dope. It wasn't a perfect scenario for a controlled buy, but I wanted the dealer and this was the only informant I had at the time who could even get close to him.

My partner and I gave our C.I. money and drove him to his friend's apartment. We were parked a short distance away from the front of her apartment and we watched the dealer arrive. He went inside and met our informant. He sold him dope and the informant returned to our car where we were waiting. Later, when I wrote the probable cause for the search warrant, it was obvious that if the suspect had a copy of the affidavit and read the details surrounding the controlled buy, he would know who was working for us. This dealer had a reputation for violence and I was afraid for my informant's safety. I attached a Hobb's Order with my search warrant affidavit and protected the probable cause that would jeopardize my informant's confidentiality and it protected his identity.

Hobb's Orders are specific to protecting confidential informants and they are typically used in dope search warrants. Above is only one scenario where a portion of the probable cause in the search warrant affidavit needs to be concealed in order to protect someone. In sexual assault cases, child pornography, and other types of investigations, there are times when it will be necessary to protect victims instead of dope informants. You can request portions of the search warrant affidavit probable cause be sealed given nearly any situation as long as you can justify the need for keeping information confidential. Remember, once you have completed your search warrant and returned it to the court, it can be obtained as a public record. Anyone can get a copy of it and the information contained within. Save yourself later problems by recognizing ahead of time what information you don't want the public, and especially your suspect, to know.

## SEIZING AND RELEASING EVIDENCE

When you seize evidence pursuant to a search warrant, that evidence is supposed to be taken to the Magistrate who ordered the search warrant execution. Now, that doesn't literally mean you are going to take a bag of dope with paraphernalia and dump in on the judge's desk. It does mean, however, that you cannot release items of evidence seized pursuant to a search warrant without an order from the judge. If you expect to seize very large items of evidence, such as tables and chairs, and those items belong to a victim of a crime such as a burglary, you can request authorization beforehand that you may photograph the items seized and then release those items of evidence at the location of the search warrant.

Typically, in most search warrants, you are going to seize and book everything illegal you find. You will write a receipt listing everything you seized and from where you seized it. Once your case is adjudicated, you will need a court order authorizing you to release property seized during a search warrant. Let's say, for example, you served a dope search warrant and seized a bunch of dope, a scanner, and video surveillance equipment. Once the case goes to court and is adjudicated, you will need to release the items of evidence you seized that are not illegal for someone to possess. Naturally, you aren't going to give an ounce of dope back to your suspect, but you need to release the scanner and cameras that are not illegal to own. Unlike a normal property release, those items seized during the search warrant will need to be ordered released by the judge.

## PREPARE NOW

The best time to start your preparation for your search warrant is now. Now you have the time to get a template and start filling in the blanks with your information. Now is the time to prepare your expertise and have it written into a blank search warrant document. Do your research ahead of time and know what format your department uses. Get a copy of a Hobb's Order and put it in your search warrant file. Get copies of other's search warrants and read through them. Ask your partners who have done search warrants how they did them and if you are so inclined, write a practice search warrant and get used to the format. If you take the time to start familiarizing yourself with the process and you get your documents organized and accessible now, you will be better prepared for your first search warrant when the time comes. It is better to have your questions answered now, than at three o'clock in the morning some day when timeliness is important.

Don't be afraid of the judge. He is there to help you do your job. I haven't met a judge who wasn't supportive of my efforts to get a search warrant as part of a criminal investigation. I have had judges tell me they won't authorize a search based on the probable cause as I had it written at the time. With some additional information and different word choice, those search warrants were eventually authorized. Because I know judges sometimes like to change things, I always take a disc of the search warrant with me so I can make those changes at the court house and not have to return to my office. I have never had a search warrant request completely rejected. Once you have established rapport with some judges, ask them about search warrants and what they like them to contain. I have met some judges who prefer a different format because of style. You only learn sometimes through trial and error. As with the under-the-influence arrest, the more search warrants you write the better you will get and the more expertise you will gain.

# Chapter Eleven
## The Ruse

### WE CAN LIE?

It's amazing how many crooks believe the cops cannot lie to them during an interview. Well, we can. And, we can use this common belief to our benefit during interviews. The ruse, when used within the law and with finesse, is one of the most effective investigative tools we have available to us during all types of investigations. It is foremost in my mind when I am interviewing a suspect I know will not be truthful unless he thinks I know the truth about what happened. Aside from a video surveillance tape or an un-involved third party eyewitness who has no motivation to lie, how many times do we get to know the truth about what happened? We can have an idea and an educated guess, but without a confession from the suspect or at least a partial admission, we never get the whole truth. The effective use of a ruse, however, can help you get closer to the truth. In order for a ruse to be legal, it must be something believable and not so extreme that it would make an otherwise innocent person confess to something he didn't do. It must be used with the intent of finding the truth, not a confession. Here are a couple examples of some simple ruses I have used during different investigations and one complex and detailed ruse my partner and I used during a drug investigation.

## THE 911 PRANKSTER

I was working a night shift in a rural part of the western end of our county. My beat covered so many square miles it could take me over forty minutes to drive from one part of the area to the next for a call for service. Most of the calls were localized, but every now and then we got called to the outskirts for something. During a two week period, about three or four times a week, the late night shifts would get a 911 call from an oilfield business outside of town. It took at least twenty minutes to drive there and each time we arrived we found the 911 calls were false. It was obvious there was a prankster calling for his late night entertainment. We were all getting annoyed at these calls and I chose to make the prankster my entertainment for the evening.

The last time I got a 911 call from the business, which was a large plant with about a hundred telephone lines and a thousand employees working there, I decided to solve the problem and make sure we never got another false report from there. The caller told dispatch to, "Hurry, there's a man down!" And then he hung up and didn't answer dispatch's return call. They gave me the address to the plant and an outlying building number where the call came from. I asked dispatch to play the 911 call for me and I listened to the man myself. He was speaking in a quiet voice. He was older and he sounded like he was in his mid forties. He also spoke with a Spanish accent.

That night I had a partner working with me. She too had responded to the plant a couple of times for 911 calls and this time, instead of driving straight to the plant and looking for a man down, I stopped about a mile or two before we arrived and I made myself a "throw down" fingerprint card. Those of us working in rural substations processed our own crime scenes and we all had our own fingerprint dusting kits assigned. I popped my trunk and removed my dust kit. I rubbed my index finger on the side of my nose and lathered it with some good old "magic oil." I put my oiled finger down on my trunk lid and used my brush to dust the powder and reveal the perfect print. I lifted the print and put it on a fresh fingerprint card. It was CSI quality and would have made Hollywood proud! I put the print in my pocket, told my partner the plan, and we headed to the call.

We drove around the facility for awhile until we found the outbuilding from where the call came. Inside, we found two night janitors sitting in the break room. I told them we received a 911 call from there and asked them if there was an emergency. They both said there was no emergency and one, an older Hispanic man in his mid forties who spoke with a Spanish accent, was especially helpful to add he didn't see anyone use the phone. Well, I recognized his voice and I could have easily made a misdemeanor case against him, written a report and all, but that wouldn't have been any fun. No, it was our turn for entertainment at his expense.

There were five or six different phone lines in the building and I asked dispatch to call the number where the 911 came from and they did. A phone in the far corner rang and the moment seemed like one from an Alfred Hitchcock movie. There was painful silence and as the phone rang we all stood there looking at it and each other. I told the two men, "I guess that's the phone that was used, huh?" They both shrugged their shoulders and agreed. Armed with my latent fingerprint evidence waiting in my pocket, I asked my partner to go to her car and get her fingerprint kit.

While she was getting her kit from her car, I told the men that reporting a false emergency and the misuse of 911 was a felony, of course, and punishable by five years in prison. I told them about the new legislation passed in January that made the false report a felony. I told them the story about the ambulance driver and paramedic who were killed responding to a false emergency someone reported as a hoax and as a result "David's Law" was passed making it a felony and so on. I told them I was going to dust the phone for fingerprints and then compare the prints I found to theirs. I said I was certain neither of them made the call so they need not be alarmed. But, since they were the only two there, I was going to compare the prints to theirs just to eliminate them as suspects. I asked them both to get their driver's licenses so I could get their information to later compare with prints filed with the Department of Motor Vehicles records.

I watched them fumble through their wallets to find their driver's licenses and the older Hispanic guy looked at me and asked, "You really going to check for prints?" "Of course," I said, "It's a felony and it's my job to investigate crimes. Why? Is that okay?" He stuttered and replied, "No, no. That's fine. I just never seen this before." I assured him, "I do it all the time. And, not to brag or anything, but I'm damn good at finding fingerprints. Sometimes it seems like I can just pull one out of my pocket when I really look."

When my partner came back inside with her print kit, I put on my latex gloves and asked her to get their information while I went to work. I whispered in her ear to keep the guys occupied while I sprinkled some magic powder on the phone and pulled out my print card. My partner knew my games and had been with me on other ruses. She started talking to them and I blocked their view of the phone by standing in front of it with my back facing them. I sprinkled the black graphite all over the place and made a fine mess. I looked over my shoulder and saw them writing their names and addresses down on my partner's notepad. I pulled my perfect, CSI quality, index fingerprint from my pocket and shouted, "Bingo!" My partner asked me, "Did you find one?" "Yes ma'am," I said and then I walked over to show her and the two employees the perfect fingerprint I lifted off the number nine on the telephone.

I took off my gloves and wrote on the fingerprint card the date and time and drew a small sketch of where I lifted the print off the telephone. I started to collect my stuff and the one employee asked me, "How long does it usually take to get the results back?" I looked at him and said, "On something as serious as this, only a day or two." And then I asked him, "Why? It's not yours now, is it?" He looked down and over at his buddy and said, "Um, well I have used that phone before. You know, to call home and stuff." I told him, "Sure, your prints should be on the phone then. What's your phone number again?" He told me and I replied, "There are no number nines in your phone number. The print I lifted came off the number nine button and it was the most recent print there. It was on top of the other fingerprints on the nine button." That didn't make him feel any better. I told him I would be in touch with his employer when I got the results back and then I would return with a warrant and arrest the person who made the call. I told them I would make the arrest in front of all his fellow employees, "Just to make a point."

My partner and I left those two standing there looking dumbfounded. We drove outside the plant's property and parked a couple of miles away where we both had a good laugh. That ruse was over five years ago and I don't believe there has been one 911 call from there since. What fun and a good example of how we used a simple ruse to solve a problem. Now, I always keep a good "throw down" fingerprint card handy to use during my investigations. Just in case!

## URINE SAMPLE

Most district attorneys are good enough to get an under-the-influence arrest filed without a urine sample as evidence. There are some, however, who will not file this type of case without a positive urine sample as a part of the package. For a while, I worked in an area where the district attorney filing our cases required a positive urine sample or he would dismiss our cases because of insufficient evidence. There was a particular drug addict in our area who we knew was responsible for several burglaries and each time we arrested him for being under-the-influence he always refused to provide a urine sample for analysis. Well, the district attorney would reject our cases and the guy walked free every time.

I knew we needed to get a urine sample from him to examine so we could get him convicted and get search terms on him for narcotics. I knew if he had probation search terms for drugs we would find some of our stolen property from recent burglaries while conducting probation searches. Of course, we would look for drugs, but keep our eyes open for stolen jewelry, lawnmowers, bikes, etc. After three arrests, this guy had not been convicted of anything and he walked around like he was untouchable. I was working patrol one night and I saw him walking in the roadway. I stopped him for the vehicle code violation. He was high and I arrested him again for being under-the-influence.

I drove him to the substation and I completed a drug evaluation on him. Like always, I asked him to provide a urine sample and he refused. I didn't try to talk him into giving a urine sample this time. Instead, I drove him to the jail and booked him like before. While he was sitting on the bench in the holding cell waiting to go through the actual booking process, I talked to the detention officer working the counter who was my friend. I had known this guy my entire career and I spoke with him away from my suspect.

I told my friend the guy I arrested was a burglar and we were trying to get him convicted of being under-the-influence so the court would give him probation with search terms. I told him the suspect never gave us a urine sample and the district attorney always dismissed the cases for lack of evidence. I asked my friend for a favor. I asked him to go through the booking questions and then tell the guy he needed to get a urine sample to test him for communicable diseases. I coached my friend and told him to tell the suspect it was new jail policy that every inmate booked into the county jail had to give a urine sample so the jail staff could help prevent the spread of disease and infection. I told him to tell the suspect if was for his own protection. I gave my buddy the urine kit and he walked my suspect back to a toilet.

The suspect fell for it and when he thought he was giving a urine sample for his own safety, he pissed like he'd been holding on to it like money. My friend seized the sample from him and when the guy was booked and out of sight, he gave the urine sample to me. I listed my friend in my report under the chain of evidence and submitted the case like all of the others. This time, the district attorney filed the case, the urine tested positive for amphetamines, and the guy was convicted of the drug charge and got probation with search terms. A few months later, we found him in possession of stolen property and solved several burglaries. He was sent to prison for sixteen months. I later asked the judge who convicted him if using a ruse to obtain evidence was legal. I told him how I got the urine sample from the guy by telling him it was to test for diseases not the presence of drugs. The judge loved it and told me what I did was legal and admissible.

## FEDERAL CASE

One of my more elaborate ruses came impromptu after a guy my partner and I had been watching during a drug investigation was arrested in a nearby town for drug charges. About a week before the guy was arrested, a cop from another city, who was one of my partner's friends, called her and told her about a guy named David. He learned from an informant David was involved in transporting drugs from a dealer in our area into his. The day before David was arrested, we drove by his house and took photographs of his house and car so we knew what vehicle to watch for driving around our town.

We learned from one of our informants someone was selling meth from a rural farmhouse outside of town. At the time, we didn't know where the house was or who was involved. We believed David was delivering meth from our town into the next town. We knew most drug trafficking occurred late at night and on a couple of main back roads leading into our area. Our plan was to spend several hours over the next couple of weeks and make traffic stops late at night on those back roads. We were particularly hopeful to find David's car and stop him leaving our town and heading home to his.

Before we got very far in our surveillance and investigation and the next night after we photographed David's house and car, the small police department about thirty minutes drive from our town arrested him for drug sales. We learned David was found in possession of several "eight balls" after he fled from officers on his bicycle. David was on parole and we knew he would be violated and sent back to prison. We needed to interview him before he was sent away while he was still at the local agency's jail. My partner and I thought he wouldn't tell us anything unless we had something to offer him in return. I came up with an idea.

I decided to put together a fictitious federal case against him for drug trafficking. I wanted the case to look convincing and compel David to cooperate with us for leniency on a case that didn't exist. I knew it was a long shot, but what the heck? The worst case scenario was that he'd know it was all crap and tell us to pound sand. I made another "throw down" fingerprint card and our fictitious case started there. My partner created a fake AFIS letter that showed his fingerprint was identified as the one submitted to the crime lab for analysis. I grabbed a blank VHS tape and made an evidence label with David's name printed on the front. My partner made up a fictitious photographic line-up with David's picture circled and signed by some Hispanic guy. Then, I wrote a fictitious federal Ramey Warrant in the amount of $500,000 dollars for David's arrest for drug trafficking. To make it all look official, my partner and I created the acronym CDET, or California Drug Enforcement Taskforce, and she made a very official looking cover letter we glued on an empty manila envelope to carry all of our evidence into the interview room.

It took us about an hour to put our case together and come up with a story that sounded good enough to hopefully convince David to talk. After midnight, when there were no calls pending, we drove to the jail where David was waiting to be transported to court the next morning. I told the sergeant there what I wanted to do and assured him we would not talk about his department's recent arrest and interfere with their investigation. We prepared the interview room and laid our fictitious case folder on the table. They brought David in handcuffed and he looked like a scared caged animal.

I told David it was the jail's policy that he be handcuffed during an interview. I told him that if he was cooperative, I would violate the policy and take the handcuffs off him if he'd like. He wanted the cuffs removed and my partner and I began our journey toward building his confidence and becoming his friend. I introduced us as deputies from CDET. I asked him if he'd heard of CDET before and he said, "Yeah, I think I've heard of you guys." I gave him a short history about how CDET began as a grant project when Governor Schwarzenegger was elected to office and he authorized a multi-agency task force to combat mid level drug dealers in rural towns and communities. David asked us, "If you guys are with CDET, then how come you're in uniform?" I replied, "That's a good question. Normally, we are dressed in plain clothes and we work undercover. However, earlier tonight, we were working the interstate as part of a uniformed drug interdiction taskforce. So, we had to shave and put our uniforms back on."

David had definitely been around the game for a while. He was in his late thirties and he sported tattoos that told his story of having been a member of the Aryan Brotherhood. His prison tattoos were already starting to fade. His sunken cheeks and his lanky body showed nearly twenty years of hard drug use. I felt our odds of pulling this ruse off were about twenty percent. But, David was inquisitive and so we kept our story and moved forward. He wanted to know why we wanted to talk to him and he asked us, "What do you got on me?" I told him I hoped he would help us in our investigation and the ruse began.

I told him that a few weeks ago we arrested a Mexican guy with a little over an ounce of methamphetamine on him. We removed the plastic covering the dope and lifted a fingerprint off the package. I pulled out the fingerprint card from our folder and showed it to him. I told him we sent the fingerprint to the lab for a fingerprint search and it matched his. My partner showed him the AFIS letter identifying him as the owner of the finger print. The AFIS letter said there was a 99.9999 percent chance in five trillion that the print didn't belong to David. Next, I told him that once we learned about him, we showed the Mexican guy we arrested a photographic line-up and he identified David as the person who was involved in drug trafficking. We showed him the line-up and told him the Mexican guy already took a deal for his testimony. I told him we taped the interview to use later for court and I showed him the VHS tape. I told David the guy was probably already back in Mexico by now.

I had taken digital photographs of some electronic items I had listed for sale on eBay. One of the items was a box called "The Hum Eliminator." I used to play music in nightclubs and I used the box to cut hum from my guitar so it didn't come through the PA system. The box was black and had ¼ inch jack inputs on each side. It looked like something official that I could use so I printed a copy of it with the pictures of David's house we took the night before. I showed David a photograph of his house with his car in the driveway. He looked at the photo and said, "That's my house!" I asked him if he recognized the car and he said, "Yeah, that's my car!" He asked, "You took those pictures?" And I told him, "No, this did." I dropped an 8x10 photograph of my "Hum Eliminator" that hadn't yet sold on Ebay and I crossed my fingers and hoped David wasn't a guitar player.

I asked him if he knew what a "Hum Eliminator" was used for. He didn't and I told him if was a wireless device that records both audio and video signals from remote locations. I told him it was quite expensive, but CDET had a big budget and a lot of cool toys. There was a park across the street from David's house and I asked him if he remembered about a week ago seeing a lawn maintenance guy trimming the tree branches. He thought for a second and said, "Yeah, I think so." I told him the guy trimming the tree actually was a member of CDET and he installed the "Hum Eliminator" in the tree pointing it toward his house. It had been there taking pictures of all the cars coming and going from his house.

David sat there speechless for a moment and I didn't want to overwhelm him and make it seem like we had too much intelligence on him, so I told him to, "Think about all of this for a minute and I'll be back." I asked him if he liked Dr.Pepper and he said, "Yeah." I told him I would be right back and bring him one. My partner and I left all of our evidence on the table knowing full well David was going to look through it. We left for about five minutes and took a short strategic break. We had already been in the interview room with David for close to an hour and we hadn't yet asked him for his help. We also hadn't yet fully laid our case out for him to see. We were having a grand time and I started to think our ruse was going to work. It was obvious David was up to his neck in dope and not once had he denied any involvement in drug trafficking.

We watched through a two-way mirror as David looked through our evidence. He kept shaking his head and running his hand through his hair and covering his mouth. He was showing some good "defeatist posture" and I knew it was time to go back in the room and confront him with a little more evidence and the Ramey Warrant. I bumped the wall and made some noise just before we opened the interview room door. David heard us coming and tried to put everything back in the folder. I walked in the room and handed him the Dr.Pepper. I paused for a minute and asked him, "You didn't open the folder did you?" "Oh no," he said and changed the subject thanking me for the soda.

I told David we had a warrant for his arrest for federal drug trafficking charges. I asked him if he had ever been to Fort Leavenworth, Kansas and he said, "No." Leavenworth was the only federal prison I could think of off the top of my head. I told him it was a federal prison and it was where he was going. I told him federal sentences require you complete eighty percent of the sentence before you can be paroled. Therefore, I did the math for him and told him he was looking at eight to ten years after he completed his state time for the current violation he picked up earlier that day. I told him I had an offer for him I didn't think he could refuse. I told him I couldn't do anything about the new state case he just got arrested for today. I told him I did have connections with the federal judge who issued the Ramey Warrant and with his cooperation we could make the federal case go away.

David was now interested in the case and asked us, "What do you want me to do?" I told him I wanted to know where he was purchasing the drugs from the nearby town and from whom. He said, "You got a piece of paper?" We gave him a piece of paper and a pencil and he drew us a map of the house with the address, wrote down the dealer' name, phone number, listed in the map where the guy hid his dope, where the video surveillance cameras were attached to the house and what areas they covered. David told us where the guy kept his pistol and told us everything about the operation. By the time David got finished with his map and all of the information he thought we needed to know, I couldn't think of any questions to ask him. He included more detail than I would have thought to ask if I had to pry answers from him. Once he finished, he asked, "How's that?" I said, "Good." He asked if we were going to make those federal chargers go away. I told him, "Just a minute. Let us make a phone call." My partner made a fictitious call to the judge in front of David and she told the judge David was cooperative and she asked if we could disregard the Ramey Warrant. The judge was agreeable and I tore the warrant in half in front of David. Then, we destroyed some of our evidence and threw it in the trash can for him to see our "good faith." As we put the handcuffs back on him and thanked him for his cooperation, he said, "It's good to work with people who can do things." Oh David, yes it is!

We walked out of the interview about an hour and a half later in disbelief we pulled off that ruse. When we got back to our area, we found the house David told us about and verified everything he said. The guy who lived there was on probation for drugs and for the next week we watched the house and made several good felony possession arrests leaving there. Eventually, we hit the house and arrested the guy for drug sales. The dope, cameras, gun, and everything else we needed for a good sales case was exactly where David said it would be. We seized an ounce of methamphetamine and about a thousand dollars in cash. We found pay and owe sheets, scales, packaging material, a loaded 9mm pistol, and a decent video surveillance set up. We arrested five people from the house and sent the dealer to prison for drug sales. Not a bad hook considering the information about the house came from a completely fictitious case and a ruse that took us only a few hours to pull off, eh?

# INVESTIGATIVE TECHNIQUE

Whether you are investigating juveniles who burglarized the local elementary school or conducting a drug investigation, the ruse is only limited to your imagination. It is a powerful investigative technique and tool that when used effectively, can help you find the truth. Remember, in order for it to be legal, it must not be so outrageous to make an otherwise innocent person admit to something he didn't do. Depending on the type of investigation you are conducting, it can be something as simple as telling a person you have a video tape of the crime. If the person wasn't there and didn't do anything wrong, he is going to tell you, "Great! When you watch it, you'll see it wasn't me." The guilty person, however, is going to start to worry about what's on the tape.

Be creative in your ruses and have fun with them. I have used spa test strips that check for the Ph levels and bromine in the water and told a suspect it was a test kit used to determine drug levels in a person. Once, I had a doper who I knew had used but he wouldn't admit his drug use to me. I took one of my spa test strips and rubbed it on the sweat from his forehead. I told him the sweat would show the presence of methamphetamine and after I told him the test positively confirmed he had meth in his system, he admitted to smoking earlier. Anything can be used as a ruse. Make it part of your game plan during an investigation. It should be in your mind before you begin an interview with a suspect. Ask yourself what small trick you can use to help you get the truth. When you start to be prepared, your interview results will improve.

As I have mentioned many times throughout this book, in order to be effective and become a good street-level dope cop, you have to start to think "outside the box." You aren't doing anything illegal and you're not being crooked. You are just being smart. You are using uncommon techniques to solve common problems. When you can embrace a problem and look forward to finding an unorthodox solution, you will start to improve. You will take on a leadership role amongst your partners and the smart ones will want to align themselves with you. If your partners start to develop with you, together you will be able to solve nearly any law enforcement problem. And that is a wonderful feeling.

# Chapter Twelve
## The Criminal Process

## COURT

Although going to court may not be your ultimate goal, it is a fact that every arrest you make will eventually end up in court. I am a proponent of not worrying about what happens in court and what the district attorney does with the case. Even if you make a seemingly pointless arrest based on state laws or your department's policy, that arrest will at least go to arraignment before it is dismissed. It is our right as American citizens to have our day in court and all police officers will be under subpoena as a witness at some point in their careers. Inevitably, the more people you arrest and the more work you do, the more time you will spend in court. Therefore, I have included this chapter not as a comprehensive guide to courtroom procedures, but as a general reference. It is important that police officers have a working knowledge of the court processes so they can better understand their roles as witnesses.

# ARRAIGNMENT

Within forty-eight hours after you have arrested a person he has the right to appear before a Magistrate to have the charges heard. Every person you arrest who is not either cited out with a promise to appear in court at a later date or who has posted bail, will appear in court at an arraignment within forty-eight hours. The arraignment period includes two working court days. So, if you arrest someone on a Friday evening and court is closed on Monday because of a holiday, that person will be in court Tuesday morning. Granted, it is not within forty-eight hours of the arrest, but within the spirit of the law, he gets to court as soon as possible.

Although the judge only needs your probable cause to determine if the charges are substantiated enough to bound a person over for trial, the court clerk needs your report for the complaint packet. It is imperative you have your report written by then so the suspect doesn't get released. There will be a time in your career, I promise, when the court will be looking for your report and you'll get a nasty phone call at nine o'clock in the morning after a graveyard shift with a frantic clerk screaming, "Where's your report? We need it!" So, make sure if you have a felony in custody who doesn't post bail, you get that report done before you go home.

At the arraignment, the judge reads the probable cause declaration and determines if he finds enough cause to believe the person committed the alleged offense. At misdemeanor arraignments in my county, there is no district attorney present and the judge does not have your report. Everything at this point is based solely on your probable cause declaration. This is one of the many reasons it is important to not cut corners when writing your probable cause for the arrest. Although you don't need to list minute details, you do need to be specific enough to cover the elements of the crime.

If the judge finds your probable cause adequate, he asks the suspect to plea to the charges and allegations made against him. The suspect can plea guilty, not guilty, or no contest. The first two pleas are straight forward. However, a suspect can plea no contest. This is the same as a guilty plea. The difference is it allows the person to avoid admitting guilt. For some reason, people don't want to admit they did something wrong and say, "I'm guilty. I did it." A no contest plea means, "I'm not saying I'm guilty. I'm just saying I don't want to fight this." It is a softer way of pleading guilty.

Typically, the best "deal" offered to the suspect is during the arraignment. If the suspect pleas guilty there, he will likely get the best offer for sentencing than if he fights it and goes to a jury trial. It depends on the judge and how your courtroom operates. In our metropolitan area where hundreds of people appear in court weekly for misdemeanor arraignments, there are probation officers who screen the complaints and offer the deals through probation before a judge looks at the case and allows the person to enter his plea. Regardless of where you work, the process will be similar and the arraignment is the first step a suspect goes through in the court process.

## PRE TRIAL OR PRELIMINARY HEARING

Your first court appearance will be in the pre-trial or preliminary hearing. They are the same the only difference being a pre-trial is for misdemeanor arrests and a preliminary hearing is for felonies. Regardless, this will be the first time you will get a subpoena for court. Many times, on felony matters, there will be a pre-preliminary hearing and the defendant will accept a deal and plea. Then, you will not have to go. Typically, you will only know the plea happened if you check the court case synopsis in the computer yourself the day before your scheduled court appearance. I can't count how many times I have gone to court only to find out the suspect pled the day before. And, I wasn't called and told to cancel.

What you wear to court depends on your department's policy. I typically wear my uniform to the preliminary hearing because I know there is no jury. Aside from the general public allowed in the courtroom, this hearing is held before the judge, the attorneys, and the defendant. If the defendant hasn't yet entered a plea, you will testify during the preliminary hearing. So, be sure to have your report with you and make sure you have read it and are familiar with it. There is nothing more awkward than sitting on the witness stand and continually referring to your report during the direct questioning by the district attorney. There are some specific details you just won't remember and you will have to refer to your report. If you can limit the times you refer to your report, it will make your testimony smoother and easier not only for you but for the district attorney questioning you.

During the preliminary hearing, you will be able to see the case somewhat "laid out" and you'll have an understanding of the defense. Sometimes, your probable cause for the stop will be the main focus of the preliminary hearing. Even if your stop was one hundred percent legal and good, the defense attorney might attack it because he has nothing else to use as a defense. Upon the completion of the preliminary hearing, you'll know if there is going to be a suppression motion to try and have your stop or probable cause thrown out.

## SUPPRESSION MOTION

When you make an on-sight arrest, your probable cause for the stop is your bread winner. If you had to break your report down into sections, I would say over fifty percent of your report should describe your probable cause for the stop. I'd say the other half should be divided into your evidence and the suspect's statements. The rest is mostly unimportant. If you go to court for a suppression motion, you can expect your stop to be the only thing discussed. The evidence you found after the stop including the suspect's admission or confession is irrelevant. If the defense attorney can get your stop or initial contact thrown out and ruled inadmissible, everything that happened afterward will also be thrown out. In essence, your case won't exist anymore. In the academy they talked about the exclusionary rule and the "fruits of the poisonous tree." The suppression motion is normally where this "poisonous fruit" gets thrown out of court.

For about five months during my career, I sat in court as a bailiff. I had worked patrol for about ten years before I transferred to the courts and I had been to court as a witness probably a hundred times. Being able to watch the court process as a bailiff, I learned, unfortunately from other officer's mistakes, what not to do. I remember listening to an officer sitting in the witness stand during a suppression motion and I watched as the defense attorney pointed out all of the mistakes the guy made before and during the stop. The young officer had only worked for his department for about six months and the defense attorney had been around for about twenty years. He literally ate that poor cop alive and I truly felt sorry for him as he sat there squirming in his seat feeling incompetent and stupid.

The officer lost his composure only a couple of times and to his credit, he did quite well considering how out maneuvered he was and the number of mistakes he made during a simple possession arrest and investigation. As I sat there listening, I realized I had made some of the same mistakes in my career and fortunately I never had those mistakes exploited like this young guy was currently experiencing. I made a bunch of mental notes, however, and when I returned to patrol I was better armed and I learned a few things about what can happen at court. What I basically learned was to not cut corners. I learned to be uncharacteristically thorough, especially on cases that appear to be "slam dunk."

## READINESS HEARING

If the probable cause for your stop is admissible and you "win" the suppression motion, the case could proceed to trial. More often than not, if you win the suppression motion, the suspect will enter a plea and the case will not go to trial. Sometimes, the suspect is adamant the case goes to jury trial despite having lost at the suppression motion and he will take it all the way "to the box." If the case goes that route, there will be a readiness hearing before the trial. The officer doesn't attend the readiness hearing. It will take place with just the judge, the attorneys, and sometimes the defendant if he is in custody. Again, the district attorney will likely reiterate the state's offer and try to get the suspect to enter a plea to avoid a trial. He usually does this by telling the defense he is ready to go to trial and will ask for the maximum sentence when the suspect is found guilty. It is a game and the attorneys bring their poker faces with them to court and try to call each other's bluff. From my short stay in court, I saw the defense win as much as the prosecution. The winner was usually decided at the time the officer wrote the report and when the arrest was made. Whoever has the best evidence and case usually wins. If neither concedes, the case goes forward to trial.

## THE JURY TRIAL

County deputies who work court services for a portion of their careers have a huge advantage over city cops and other officers who only see court from the witness stand. Deputies get a well rounded perspective about court and what happens through the court process. They get to know the judges and attorneys and get tremendous insight into what really happens "behind the scenes." If you are a new deputy just out of the academy, don't hate your time working in court services; embrace it. Pay attention to what happens and learn from other officer's mistakes. Take the time to understand what is happening. Don't sit in the courtroom text messaging your buddies and dreaming about working the streets. It will happen soon enough. In fact, it will probably happen too soon.

The last phase in the court process is the jury trial. If everything else has been expended and the suspect demands a trial by jury, he will get one. It is our constitutional right and it does happen, although not as often as you'd think. I'd say less than ten percent of the cases filed with the court actually make it to jury trial. But if one does go to trial, typically, the officer is the first witness for the prosecution. Before he takes the stand, however, there are tons of administrative papers filed with the court and the attorneys have written and prepared "motions in limine" or motions before the trial starts. Typically, these are motions to exclude evidence. Once all of the jury instructions are filed and the motions have been heard, the first thing that occurs is jury selection.

## JURY SELECTION

During jury selection, the attorneys get to ask the prospective jurors questions during what is called "voir dire." This is French and means "to speak the truth." During this phase of questioning, the attorneys start to eliminate jurors who they think will harm their case or not be "un biased." The attorneys get "peremptory challenges" where they can eliminate up to ten protective jurors each for no reason when they feel the juror is unfavorable to them and harmful to their case. When I sat in court, I loved to listen to "voir dire." The best thing about it was seeing the number of jurors who truly didn't want to be there. They would try everything to get eliminated from the jury so they could either go home or back to work. Some of the excuses the jurors came up with for why they could not participate were truly ingenious. Others were just stupid.

I remember getting a jury panel one afternoon and I listened to a man talking with another juror. The guy was obviously Hispanic and he spoke with an accent. His English, however, was better than mine. He was clearly educated and had been in this country for the majority of his life. He was laughing and joking and was jovial. His vocabulary was exceptional and I admired his intellect. He looked like he was financially well off and was knowledgeable about a number of different topics. About thirty minutes later while he was sitting in the courtroom during jury selection, his demeanor changed and he wasn't the confident, well spoken man I heard just minutes before.

The judge asked the prospective jurors if any of them had difficulty understanding the English language. This man now raised his hand and spoke with a Spanish accent so thick I could barely understand him. He used the wrong tense of verbs and stumbled through his words. He told the judge how, "I no speak, eh, English not good. I understand no little." The judge told him and all of the jurors how the proceedings could only be held in English and it was important for all of the jurors to be able to participate. The judge asked the man if he understood everything he said up to this point. The man was smart enough to not answer. He just stood there looking at him confused. The judge asked the man again if he understood what he just said and the man replied, "No. Not too much." Watching him and listening to him, you would have thought he just crawled across the border and was a field laborer. Well, the judge dismissed him and told him to return to jury services and tell them he'd been excused. The man understood enough English to leave the courtroom and return to jury services where he was excused. Some of the smarter jurors who paid attention during this man's performance stood up and told the judge how they too, "No, speak, eh, very good." And they were excused.

The best performance I saw was from an older woman who was smart enough to not even lie to the judge. It was during a driving under-the-influence jury trial and the judge asked the jurors if any of them had a problem with that subject matter. This lady just started crying. She didn't have to say anything. She sat there and bawled like a little baby. Well, the judge made a record for the court and said the juror obviously had a problem with the subject matter based on her emotional reaction after the question and she was dismissed. Brilliant! I was amazed at the ability of some of the jurors to "pull one over." This woman didn't even have to lie. After that Oscar performance, if a juror asked me how to get out of jury duty, I told him to just start crying when the judge asks a question. Once the sometimes "comedy of errors" known as the jury selection process is complete, the attorneys give their opening statements.

## OPENING STATEMENT

Since the state has the "burden of proof," the district attorney gives his opening statement first. An opening statement is the attorney's opportunity to explain what the case is about and how he is going to prove or disprove the suspect's guilt or innocence. The attorneys do not present evidence in the opening statement and it is more of a chance for them to tell the jurors what happened. It allows the attorneys to let the jury know who they are and how they present themselves. They do not argue their case during the opening statements. They might tell the jury who they are going to call as witnesses and how the case will be presented.

After the district attorney has given his opening statement, the defense will be allowed to give his. When they are done, the judge will ask the district attorney to call his first witness. Usually, this is the arresting officer. If you are the arresting officer, it will be your turn to take the witness stand and testify. During a jury trial, I recommend you wear a suit and not your uniform. If you are on duty working and don't have time to change, obviously you'll have to wear your uniform. The phase of questioning by the attorney who summoned you as a witness is called direct questioning.

## DIRECT QUESTIONING

Direct questioning is less stressful because you are not being "grilled." Almost always, you are the district attorney's witness. Therefore, the DA will ask questions that are easy to answer and straight forward. The DA will not try to confuse you and all you have to do is wait for the question to be posed and then answer. Try not to ramble and go into too much detail. The DA will prompt you to answer the questions and likely you'll understand what point he is trying to make. Don't be curt with your responses, because that makes you look like you are trying to hide something. As you are answering the questions, look at the jury as much as possible. After all, your testimony is for them, not the attorney. Acting normal and comfortable on the witness stand takes time and experience. It is a balancing act between looking at the jury, the attorneys, and being as normal and comfortable as possible. The time you need to be more cautious and aware of your verbal and non verbal communication is during the cross examination.

## CROSS EXAMINATION

Most of the "fireworks" we see and hear during television shows and movies happens during the cross examination. This is when the brilliant attorney gets to drill the witness and make him "crack" under the pressure. This is the most stressful time as a court witness and the time when you need to be the most cautious about what you say and how you say it. During the cross examination, the questions will usually be posed in a manner that require a "yes" or "no" response. A good defense attorney will ask you questions that if you answer only "yes" or "no" will make you look incompetent or like a liar. It is important to understand this and be careful when you do answer. Sometimes, you can answer questions like this. There are times, however, when you can't answer a question truthfully with merely a "yes" or "no" response. The way to maneuver around this is to tell the attorney, "I can't answer that question truthfully by saying 'yes' or 'no." Then, the judge will usually ask the attorney to re-phrase the question.

You are going to get frustrated during cross examination. It is inevitable. The thing to remember is you must maintain your composure and not become defensive. Getting into an argument with a defense attorney during cross examination is a huge victory for him. Showing your anger at him in front of the jury is better than telling the jury you're an idiot. The jury scrutinizes everything you do and say when you are on the witness stand and if you think you are in the "fish bowl" when you are working the streets driving a patrol car in uniform, wait until you are on the witness stand during cross examination.

If things are muddled and confused during the cross examination, the district attorney has a chance for "re-direct." This is the time for him to try and rebuild anything destroyed or confused during the cross examination. This can go back and forth until the attorneys feel they have accomplished their goal with you on the witness stand. It is normal to feel incompetent your first few times testifying in court under cross examination. When you understand and accept the fact that you are human and you are going to make mistakes, testifying in court will become much easier. If you make a mistake and that mistake is pointed out to you by the defense attorney while you are on the stand, instead of trying to "fix things," admit to the mistake and move on. If you agree with him that you have done something wrong, acknowledge the mistake and don't try and hide from it. If the attorney tries to exploit it and he keeps hammering you about it, the judge will usually tell the attorney his questions are "cumulative" or "asked and answered," meaning he has already asked that and received a response. The judge will then tell the attorney to move forward with his questioning.

When you are being questioned on cross examination, don't answer the questions too quickly. Give the district attorney a chance to object to a certain line of questioning. If you blurt out responses too fast, the jury is going to hear your response even if the district attorney objects. If the judge tells the attorney an objection is "over ruled," that means you are supposed to answer the question. If the judge says the objection is "sustained," that means you are not to answer the question and another question must be posed or the question that was "sustained" must be reworded. When I am on the stand, I get confused sometimes about "over ruled" and "sustained." I use this mnemonic to help me remember the two. If I hear the judge say an objection is "over ruled," then I think of the letter "O" and it is "okay" to answer the question. If I hear an objection is "sustained," that means the letter "S" and to "shut up." It might seem stupid, but when you are on the stand under the stress of cross examination, every little trick helps.

## CLOSING ARGUMENTS AND DELIBERATION

After the district attorney has called his witnesses forward and has presented all of the evidence in his case, the defense attorney gets to call his witnesses and present his case to the jury. Once this is done, the district attorney gives his closing argument to the jury. In the closing argument, the district attorney now gets to argue why he believes the defendant is guilty beyond a reasonable doubt and how he proved it to the jury. It is the time the district attorney explains the charges that were filed against the suspect and he gets to show the jury how and why he proved his case and that the defendant is guilty. Once he is finished, the defense attorney gets to make his closing arguments and explain why his client is innocent or why the prosecution didn't prove his client was guilty beyond a reasonable doubt. The district attorney will get to have a rebuttal closing argument and then the judge will give the jury their instructions before deliberations.

Typically, I leave the court after the jury has retired to deliberate. I don't come back for the verdict. I will usually telephone the district attorney a couple of days later and ask how the jury came back after deliberations. If the jury finds the suspect not guilty, I don't care too much. I ask the attorney why or what he thinks happened to cause the jury to find the defendant not guilty. If it was a mistake I made, I learn from it. Either way, I make certain I have done my best and that I continue to do my best in preparing my reports and during my investigations. If a jury returns a not guilty verdict in one of your cases, don't worry about it. It isn't really a loss, because you shouldn't be keeping a personal score. Do your job being a "gatherer of facts." If you always do your best, you will probably see most of your cases return with guilty verdicts.

## OFF THE STAND CONDUCT

If you are a witness for a trial that lasts a number of days and you are spending a lot of time in the court building in between your testimony, be aware of the people around you. Jurors are issued badges, but after a day or two, those badges seem to disappear and sometimes you won't know the jurors, from the defendants, and other witnesses. When you are sitting in the hallway or the break room, make certain you are on your best behavior. It is difficult when you are sitting with your beat partners to not relax and "talk shop." Whatever you do, don't talk about the case or the defendant. If jurors approach you and want to make small talk, politely tell them you can't talk to them until the trial is over and find someplace else to sit.

I was the investigating officer during one trial and while I was sitting on the bench outside the court room during a break, a juror asked me about something totally unrelated to the trial. He was just making small talk and before I could politely excuse myself from the conversation, the defense attorney walked down the hallway and saw us talking. I got up and stepped away from the juror but it was too late. The defense attorney saw an opportunity and told the district attorney and judge that I was talking to a juror. Before court could resume, I had to take the stand and tell the judge and attorneys what the juror asked me. Then, the juror was called into the courtroom and asked about the conversation as well. It was nothing, but the defense attorney moved for a mistrial and wanted to get the case up to that point thrown out of court. The judge didn't allow it and the trial went forward, but it was a bump in the road and an uncomfortable position I didn't want to find myself in again.

## BEFORE THE TRIAL

By virtue of the volume of cases they are assigned and their enormous workloads, the district attorneys sometimes will not meet with you before a trial begins. This is especially true for smaller drug cases. Naturally, if you are a witness on a homicide trial, you will have met with the attorney several times before actually taking the witness stand. But in most trials and court appearances you make, you'll probably only talk to the attorney for a few minutes immediately before you testify. Take it upon yourself to call the attorney who subpoenaed you before you actually go to court. Get an idea what they want from you and what they expect you to testify to. If you know beforehand what has happened with the case up to the point of your testimony, it will help you be better prepared. Sometimes, what you think are the important things you will testify to on the stand aren't what the attorneys are arguing. If you know for certain a case is going to trial and you'll be there for a few days, let your boss know ahead of time so he can make the necessary changes to the work schedule. Be sure to get a good night's sleep before court and take snacks and water with you. Be prepared to spend the next few days in the court building.

## BE FAMILIAR WITH THE PROCESS

You don't need to know all of the legal jargon and everything that happens in court. You only need to know the basics about what happens and what is expected of you as a witness. Aside from victims, police officers are the state's most valuable witnesses in most criminal trials. Therefore, you will go to court countless times throughout your career and having a working knowledge of the court process helps you as a witness and the district attorney prosecuting the case. As with working patrol and street-level dope, you will make mistakes while testifying in court and at trials. The import thing is to learn from those mistakes and get better. If you hear a horror story from another officer about an experience on the witness stand in court, heed what is said and make sure that same mistake doesn't happen to you. As with most things in life, the more you learn and the more you do, the better you will get and the more confidence you will have. The same is true for testifying in court. Watch others testify when you can and take from them the things they do you like and make sure you don't repeat the things they do you don't like.

# Chapter Thirteen
# Work Ethics And Integrity

## BEAT PARTNER

Have you ever heard the saying, "Great dope cops make bad beat partners?" I have too and I have worked with those types of partners. When I worked local patrol, one of my alleged beat partners was trying to make a name for himself as a great dope cop. Before we left briefing, we were already down about two report calls each. The shift before ours had been humping all day long and all they wanted was ten to fifteen minutes to woof down a burger and try to get their paper caught up. I always gathered my things quickly and made myself available for calls as soon as possible. My alleged beat partner, however, would spend an extra fifteen or twenty minutes each night at the office checking people on the computer and trying to find someone on probation to search later.

By the time my partner left the office, I was already down one report and the others had to take the calls for service that were stacking up. My partner would get to his beat area and immediately make pedestrian and traffic stops. Inevitably, he would arrest someone and spend the next two or three hours doing paperwork and trying to turn everyone he arrested into an informant. His enthusiasm for on-sight activity would have been perfect in a rural substation where there was time for self initiated activity. But in the metropolitan area, there were too many calls for service stacking up and things were way too busy to make on-sight stops. But, my partner was hell bent on making a name for himself because he wanted to go to majors and work under cover dope. He was a terrible beat partner and was selfish.

He was the type of guy who would make a traffic stop and find a little bit of dope on someone. Then, instead of just towing the car, taking the guy to jail, and booking his dope, he would make a spectacle of his arrest and broadcast to the world what a terrific job he was doing. One night, he made a stop and found some dope. He called the sergeant on the radio and asked him to go to another channel where they could talk "car to car." Well, we were all nosy so I changed over to the channel and listened to my partner's "car to car" traffic with the sergeant. He told the sergeant he found some dope and asked him to meet him at the stop. The sergeant, who was a former dope cop himself, got all excited and went to the stop.

There, they drooled over the "eight ball" my partner found and talked about ways of turning the guy into an informant and finding out where he bought the dope etc. Well, they spent a good hour at the stop and then my partner slowly made his way to the jail. Meanwhile, I went call to call and ended up writing about three reports. The units from the adjoining zone had to leave their area to back me because I didn't have a partner. There was a property room next to the jail where we could book our evidence. There was also one at the office where would could book evidence at the end of our shift if we couldn't make it to the main property room. If we booked our property at the main property room, nobody would see the evidence. So, my partner made sure he always brought his dope back to the office and he enjoyed laying out his dope and scales and packaging material all over the briefing tables for everyone to see. Inevitably, the watch commander or someone important would happen to walk by and see him with his evidence. They would always stop to see what he had and it was a great opportunity for him to advertise how wonderful he was.

Then, the next shift coming on would be in the briefing room and see what my partner had and the sergeant doing briefing would compliment him on another good proactive arrest and so on. Well, sadly some weren't smart enough to realize my partner had no integrity and while he was trying to make a name for himself, the rest of us were working twice as hard covering up for him because he was always gone on some on-sight stop. You can see the picture here and you have worked with officers like that before. So, DON'T BE THAT GUY!

## WORK ETHICS

The most important thing to consider every day when you log on and go to work is your partners. Period. Your partners come first always and once they are safe and you have taken care of them, then you can hunt and play if time allows. Every day when I started my shift, the first thing I did was call the guys working before me and find out how many reports they were down. If I had any control over it, they didn't take any more report calls while I was available. If they hadn't yet eaten their dinner, I handled the calls until they ate. I did everything I could to make their shifts a little bit better. Sometimes, they returned the gesture. But whether they did or not, that was my focus every day I went to work. Their safety and comfort came first. Always.

If I was working metropolitan patrol as part of a squad, my immediate beat partner came first. If the calls for service slowed down and we were both caught up with our reports, then I started to hunt and play. I always invited my beat partner to join me. Sometimes, I would challenge him to a little game and tell him that if he found a felony hook first, I would buy dinner. And usually he would agree to the game and if I found one first, he would buy me dinner. A good work ethic like this improves camaraderie and *esprit de corps*. Take care of each other first and worry about dope later.

## TEAMWORK

The lone ranger who is out for himself and wants all of the recognition alone is limited to what he can do. He might make a couple of good arrests, but collectively his accomplishments are small. If you have a good team of partners who all have the same objective and that objective is working street-level dope, not for self recognition, but to help clean up a community and make the quality of life better for the residents, you will have a much better chance for notable success. Here is an example of the productivity of honest teamwork.

Early one morning, I received a telephone call from an informant about a person transporting dope. I was on my days off and it was about five o'clock in the morning. I had pneumonia and was in the hospital on a respirator getting a nice dose of Albuterol and Prednisone. The informant told me about a guy named Manuel who lived in a rural farm house who had been cooking dope and bringing it into town. My informant told me Manuel had two ounces of meth in the tool box of his truck. The C.I. said Manuel was driving a beige Chevy S-10 pick-up with a white tool box on the back. She said Manuel had two ounces of meth and kept it in the tool box behind the driver's seat. He was going to deliver the dope in the morning before he went to work. She told me where he was going to deliver the dope and we were able to estimate which route he would drive.

Since I wasn't working and was in the hospital, I knew I wouldn't be able to make a stop on Manuel and do anything. Instead of letting an opportunity pass just because I wouldn't be there, I telephoned one of my partners and told him about what I just learned. My partner was an aggressive dope cop and he jumped on the chance to make a good hook. My partner knew Manuel because we had all been watching his house and we knew he was involved in the manufacturing and sales of meth. My partner parked in a almond orchard and waited for Manuel to drive passed him on the way into town to make his delivery. When Manuel drove passed, he followed him and stopped him for speeding. Manuel was under-the-influence and my partner arrested him. He did an inventory search of the truck before the tow's arrival. He found the two ounces of meth in the tool box behind the driver's seat.

After he found the dope, my partner called me and told me about the stop. I was excited and told him it would be a good time to get a search warrant for Manuel's house and look for the lab and more dope. Our sergeant agreed and they began writing the search warrant. I called my informant back and told her about the stop. I asked her about the house and she told me Manuel probably had a meth lab in the garage. She told me he buried his dope in the yard near an old water tank. She said he might have up to a pound buried there. After I spoke with my

C.I., I called my partner back and told him everything I had just learned and knew about the house.

Later that morning, he got a search warrant and put together a team. They hit the house and began their search. Just like my informant said, there was a pound of meth buried near the water tank and there was a lab in the garage. The team seized about seven firearms as well. Not too bad for a day's work, huh? This all happened and was possible because of teamwork. Had any one of us kept information to ourselves, that arrest would have never happened. True, I would have loved to have been there to kick in the door or be the one to find the dope, but I couldn't. I was sick and it wasn't my day. I did develop the informant who gave us the information that led to that successful arrest and I did give that information to my partner. So, even though I wasn't there, I was a huge part of that search warrant and arrest.

## SECRET SQUIRREL STUFF

There is a time when working dope and police work in general that information needs to be kept confidential from other cops. Sometimes, you don't broadcast what you are doing. When I develop an informant, I don't tell all of my partners the informant's name. The partner who was with me when I signed up the informant and my boss are the only two people who know. Only cops who have never worked an informant and who don't understand working dope ask, "Who's your C.I.?" Asking another cop to name his informant is like asking if your partner's daughter is still a virgin. YOU DON'T DO IT! You don't need to know who your partners are working as confidential informants.

It would be nice if everyone, especially cops, had enough integrity to keep a secret. But, we all work with partners who like to talk too much. It's not that they have mal intentions about disclosing confidential information; it's just they don't know when to keep their mouths shut. To avoid being rude, when someone asks me the name of my informant, I tell him I have it written down on my notes in my car and I can't remember off the top of my head. You're not saying, "It's none of your damn business!" You're just saying, "I'm an idiot and I don't remember. But if I could, I'd tell you." A cop with any sense about him will realize he has asked you a question he shouldn't have and he'll respect your answer.

In addition to being careful about revealing my informants, I am also careful about disclosing the location of a drug house to certain cops. If I am using a drug house as a fishing hole and we are trying to make arrests coming out of the house, I tell everyone who's interested about the house and who lives there. If I have an informant and I am about to make a controlled buy from that house and I plan on writing a search warrant and hitting it in a few days, I leave that part of the information out. Inevitably, one of your partners will get all excited there is going to be a search warrant served at that house and they will do something stupid to ruin your chances of finding dope. I have heard deputies bragging to other deputies at the Fastrip in front of the clerk whose brother is a parolee who uses dope and buys from the house we're going to hit. Then the clerk tells the brother who tells the dealer who moves etc.

I recall making a controlled buy one evening and I was nonchalant about the buy and the information about the search warrant. It seemed that on some of the other buys we had done and the search warrants we served recently, the dealers knew we were coming. I wasn't sure if we had been "burned," or if it was just a coincidence. To test the theory, I left the search warrant laying on my desk so all of my partners could read it. I made no effort to hide the fact I was going to search the house in a few days. Everybody knew about it and if someone asked me about it, I told him. I served the search warrant on the tenth day after it was signed. When I hit the house, it was empty. The tenants had moved and the only thing that remained was a bunch of spent baggies. Hmmm. How is it possible that confidential information made available only to other law enforcement officers got back to a drug dealer? Well, it does because people like to talk.

I had a good friend and trusted partner start to reveal some "secrets" to me once about a beat wife he either had been seeing or wanted to start seeing. I didn't know and I told him, "Don't tell me this. I don't want to know." He asked me, "What? Aren't you trustworthy?" I told him, "I am, but you can't trust me." He didn't understand what I meant. I told him, "Listen. I like to drink and you can't trust a drunk. I could get drunk some day and say something I shouldn't. If I don't know in the first place, I can't do any harm." I told him about secrets and if it was truly a secret, he shouldn't tell me. Think about it. If people could keep secrets, how many homicides would remain unsolved?

## PRIORITIZE AND BE HUMBLE

If you are working patrol and are assigned to a substation, a squad, or a certain shift, the partners you work with and the citizens you serve take precedent over working dope. If an old lady calls to report someone used her debit card illegally, handle that call first and give that woman one hundred percent of your time and attention. Your partner's needs and the community come first and dope second. When you go out and stop a doper, you are creating self-initiated activity. If calls are pending, handle them first.

Once you develop your skills and become an aggressive dope cop, don't become infatuated with yourself. Know you are doing a good job and be proud of the quality of work you produce. But don't become a "know it all" and look down on others who don't have your enthusiasm for dope. Not all cops work dope and like I mentioned in the first chapter when I discussed gathering intelligence, I categorized deputies who didn't work dope as generally useless. I still believe this, however I don't brag to them about my accomplishments and arrests. I don't need to make them feel less so I can feel more.

Dope cops have a tendency to "offend" people when they don't tell them about cases they are working and because they are getting a lot of arrests compared to them. Not all officers are competitive and keep track of their arrests. If they don't and you do, fine. Always include your partners to join you in your investigations and if they do, treat them well and show them you appreciate their help. Even if they didn't help much and probably made more work for you because they didn't know what they were doing, acknowledge them and make them feel useful. By virtue of your aggressiveness and the types of arrests you are making compared to them, you will take on a leadership role and they will follow you around.

If you find some of your partners following you around on your stops and calls, make an effort to teach them what you know and have learned. Your experience and life lessons shouldn't be a secret. Share them with others and try to bring others up to your level of work ethic and expertise. Think of it like the military. The sergeant's job should be to train his corporal to do his job. That way, if the sergeant is killed or injured and can't lead, the corporal can pick up the flag and move forward. He knows the mission objective and how it was going to be accomplished. The corporal, in turn, trains his subordinates to do his job and so on. If you bring your beat partners up to your level and they know what you are doing and how you are doing it, if you leave or transfer, they can continue what you started. It takes a humble and confident person to do this. But, if you work with this ethic, your partners with always appreciate you for what you have done for them and you will benefit as well.

# Chapter Fourteen
# Unorthodox Patrol Procedures

## THINKING "OUTISDE THE BOX"

I attended a four month long POST academy and I learned all of the textbook proven safe tactics and techniques all of you did or will learn in your academy. And, they are all very good to know and practice during your daily patrol duties. Simple things like using the "Interview Stance" and parking a few houses down from the address of your call and not doing building searches alone and standing off to one side of a door before knocking etc. are all wonderfully sound tactics to use and make second nature. If you work in a traditional environment with partners and on duty supervisors these tactics are great and should be used. Most, even if you are working alone, should still be used.

There are times, however, when you will find yourself working in a rural area alone or even in the metropolitan area where your back-up units are busy with other calls or arrests. It is these lonely times when your ability to talk and think "outside the box" can make the difference in determining whether or not you go home at the end of your shift. These are extreme circumstances as they pertain to basic officer survival. When working street-level dope, if you can come up with unorthodox techniques and ideas of how to hunt dopers and seize dope, your percentage of *Luck vs. Skill* will be turned again in your favor.

For most of my career, I worked substations where I was alone for either part of or all of my shift. Being alone all the time, I was able to think about many things others didn't. I was able to ask myself why time flies by when you're having fun and actually come up with a mathematical explanation. I would have the time to ponder why there are so many golf balls on the moon or how sour cream can spoil when it's already sour. I got to explore the universe and the cosmos and really understand the concept that there is life after death and so on. Yes, I had too much time on my hands and that probably wasn't healthy. But, what doesn't kill you makes you stronger. Right? One thing I did think about a lot was how to handle routine scenarios and situations alone using unorthodox techniques they didn't teach us in the academy. One scenario I thought about beforehand was how to make a high risk traffic stop alone if my nearest back-up was forty minutes away. I developed a technique I thought would be good if I was ever in that situation alone and as fait would have it, it happened. My idea worked well.

## SOLO HIGH RISK CAR STOP

Most patrol cars I have seen throughout my career are basically set up the same. The light controls, the radio, and traffic advisor are all relatively similar. Therefore, you should be able to use this technique or a modification of it with your department's equipment. The only requirements are that your car radio is capable of being broadcast through your PA system and you have a "car to car" channel or a "direct" channel. Basically, you need to be able to turn your hand held radio to that off channel and have it go through your car's PA system. The drawback is you temporarily lose contact with your dispatch. But, if you are alone and it's all or nothing, who cares about being able to talk to dispatch? All you have is yourself and if you fail, you'll be dead and talking to dispatch won't matter anyway! Here's how it works.

We have all practiced high risk or "felony" car stops as they used to be called. If you've been on patrol for any length of time you have probably been on many real high risk car stops. Well, one night I made a traffic stop on a car occupied by three suspects and that car returned as the suspect vehicle from a car jacking. My nearest back-up was going to be the highway patrol and they weren't even close. I knew I was alone for at least thirty minutes. I could have waited that long and held the car at gunpoint until a back-up unit arrived. And, I thought about that. I also knew the longer I sat there waiting, the sooner the three suspects would figure out I was alone. My fear was that the longer I waited, the more time I gave them to decide they wouldn't play fair anymore and my "temporarily controlled" high risk car stop would turn into a hornets' nest. I didn't want to find out if I could keep control and win. So, I used one of my tricks I thought about and actually practiced one night in a park (hopefully nobody was watching!)

I knew that if a gunfight erupted, the suspects were going to shoot at my car. Why? Because they all know we hide behind our cars and are talking to them with our PA from our cars. That's what cops do. We know it and they know it. So, I put both of my spotlights on their car, turned my hand held radio and car radio to an off channel, turned on my car's PA system to where the radio traffic broadcast through the siren/PA mounted on the front of my car, grabbed my shotgun out of the rack, and I ditched my car. I actually walked up along the side of the suspect's car and stood about ten yards to the side of their passenger window. I had some bushes to hide behind and I knelt down and conducted my high risk car stop from off to the side of their car.

When I looked into their car, they were all straining to block the bright spotlights and see behind them and back at my car. I held my shotgun on them and talked into my hand held microphone, "Driver! Turn off the vehicle and throw the keys ..." I had the driver exit his car and walk back to mine. When I talked into my hand held microphone, it broadcast through my car's PA speaker. It sounded like I was standing at my driver's door talking on the car microphone. I walked the driver back to my car and had him kneel down just in front of my driver's door. When I saw he was compliant, I walked from the bush, around my car, up to the driver, and handcuffed him. I searched him and tossed him in the back seat. I walked back to my hiding spot to the side of their car and did it two more times until I had arrested all three.

Had they "come out a blazing," I would have been able to take them out easily without them ever knowing what happened. My car would have been riddled with bullets. But, I wouldn't have been there hiding from a hail of lead. I was off to the side with a tremendous advantage having my street howitzer and the element of surprise. True, I didn't have the cover I would have liked. But, I believe the odds would have been stacked heavily in my favor. After I arrested the three, they couldn't believe I was alone. I found two pistols accessible in their car and overheard them talking to each other. The gist of their conversation was, had they known I was alone, they would have tried to kill me. Had I waited thirty minutes for a back-up instead of taking an aggressive, unorthodox approach, things might have been horribly different. I am confident I would have won, but the expense might have been much higher. And, I would have missed breakfast waiting for the coroner to arrive!

## PATROL DRIVING TACTICS

If you ask me, I'd tell you the next best think since sliced bread and peanut butter is the blackout switch in my patrol car. If your agency condones the use of the blackout drive and actually puts a switch in you cars so you can drive around without activating your brake lights, use it. It is true that you are liable for an accident that results from you driving without your lights activated. But, if you are smart and cautious, you can learn to drive most of your shift without turning on your headlights.

I was talking to a deputy one afternoon and I asked him how he and his partners were patrolling at night. I hadn't seen any under-the-influence arrests coming from this young group of deputies and I knew they were eager to arrest people and take them to jail. I just wasn't seeing it. He told me they drove around looking for people walking or cars to stop. I asked him, "Are you driving around with your lights on?" He kind of stared at me with a puzzled look on his face and said, "Well, yes." Maybe he thought it was a trick question and I was going to lecture him on the vehicle code and public perception and so on if he told me, "No."

I told him very simply, they weren't getting many arrests because the dopers saw them coming. If you drive around in your patrol car with your windows rolled up and your heater on full blast, and you keep hitting your alley lights and headlights, everyone within a mile is going to see you and you'll never be able to get close enough to see a crook, let alone catch him. If you keep your windows rolled up, you aren't going to hear those faint voices and the rattling trashcan or chain link fence a thug just ran into while hiding from you.

Since I hired on in the late nineties, I have driven a venerable Ford Crown Victoria as my patrol car. Sure, I've driven every model from 1992 to 2008. And I love them! But, one thing they all have in common is their uniquely custom, squeaky brakes. True, ain't it? A Crown Vic's squeaky brakes and signature V8 can be heard from several blocks away. On a nice, slow, quiet, dark night, they can be heard even further away. When you've been on foot and one of your partners have driven by or arrived at your call to back you up, I'm certain you heard them coming and knew they would be there in a moment. I've actually held off fighting a suspect until I heard that Crown Vic a couple of blocks away before I went "hands on" with my suspect. Rest assured, if you can tell a cop car coming down the road, so can dopers and crooks. In fact, their senses are more honed and they can hear you coming from far away.

Knowing this, there are some things you can do to fool them and increase your chances of getting closer to them before they hide or run. The simplest thing you can do is activate your blackout lights and drive around very slowly with your windows down and your lights off. Like I mentioned earlier in the chapter discussing surveillance, if you let your eyes adjust to the dark, you can see just fine without light. Sometimes, the moonlight alone is enough. If you work in a residential area, house lights and street lights are ample light by which you can see. If your car doesn't have a blackout switch and you need to brake and you don't want your brake lights to give you away, use your emergency brake to stop. It's awkward, but it works.

After you have heavily hunted and patrolled an area for several moths, you will have the criminals trained and they will know you drive around without your lights. They can still hear you and they'll start to hide. If you find you are having a tough time trying to catch people walking around at night and it seems things have slowed down, it's probably because they have somewhat. A trick I learned from a seasoned deputy who used to get more hooks than me is to unplug one of your front headlights. I saw him driving around one night and his passenger side headlight was out. I told him it was out and he said he unplugged it on purpose. He told me dopers don't expect you to be driving around with a headlight out. Dopers drive around like that, but not the cops.

A couple of years later, I remembered what he told me. I was working an area we had all but hunted out. A couple of my partners and I had arrested so many dopers within a few month period, it didn't seem there were any out of jail to arrest. Desperate to find someone to arrest, I popped my hood and unplugged my passenger side headlight. Within about fifteen minutes, I saw a guy riding a bicycle in the middle of the road and he had no lights on his bike. Instead of racing up to him, I just kept driving at a normal speed and I drove right up on him. I had my driver's side window down and when I got close to him, I hollered, "What's up man?" He stopped and as I was walking up to him, I heard him say, "Oh shit!" He had no idea I was a cop and he didn't expect a cop car to have a headlight out. Well, my new friend had a bag of dope in his hand and brass knuckles in his pocket. Yeehaw!

## POLICE SCANNERS

My grandmother was a good God fearing woman who loved to sit at night and read her bible and knit. My dad gave her a police scanner and for the rest of her life she kept that scanner next to her chair and listened to it as regularly as she read her bible. Unfortunately, dopers have scanners too and they use them for very different reason than my grandmother.

It never seems to amaze me how often cops forget crooks have scanners and listen to their radio traffic. Remember when Geraldo Rivera was filming his documentaries on Al Capone's vaults and later introduced the idea of cameramen riding along with police officers? (This was before COPS) Well, I do. I was watching Geraldo when he was filming live as he rode with a narcotics task force executing a search warrant at a drug dealer's house. Yes, I was watching on television, and so were the drug dealers as the team hit the house. Geraldo's camera showed them on the television inside the same house they just raided. Great! I always remembered that episode and have since been cautious of what I said on the radio just before I raided a house.

I used to work an area so thick with scanners and pagers that when the cops rolled into town, every tweaker's pager started beeping

"505050." It was always fun to stop someone, hear his pager, and see that on the screen. It was sort of like doing a probation or parole search and having the phone in the house ring off the hook with friends and neighbors saying when you answered, "Dude, there's cops at your house!" I would answer, "Really? Where? I don't see them!" One time I stopped a doper walking along the railroad tracks and I was talking into my hand held radio to dispatch as I walked up to him. I heard myself transmitting through his pocket. I searched him and he had a hand held scanner in his pocket. So, I decided it was time to use this technology to my advantage to get arrests.

Since everyone knew where I was at all times and knew I was the only deputy on duty, they knew that if I broadcast on the radio I was someplace thirty minutes away, they had at least that much time to thieve and steal and burglarize and use their dope and walk around. I called that special time their "crime spree time." Sitting alone one night, I decided to play with them and thinking "outside the box," I backed into an abandoned house that gave me a good view of the main street. I sat there for about twenty or thirty minutes and nary an insect moved. I telephoned my dispatch and told them I was going to put out a bunch of bogus radio traffic. I told them to play along but leave me available in town.

I got on the radio and asked dispatch if there were any calls pending in my area. They replied none were pending and I told them I would be out of service in the next town on follow-up investigation and if there was a call my response time would be extended. All of my nosy doper friends heard this and within about two minutes, three or four people were popping out of houses and every nook and cranny. I watched them and knew I had only one chance to pick one to stop and get an arrest. I found one and stopped him. I didn't get a felony possession arrest, but, he was high, high, high and I did get an under-the-influence arrest and, as I like to think, I prevented a burglary.

I used that trick many other times with success and passed it along to anyone who wanted to listen. Basically, I was using the doper's scanners and their technology against them. I would often give out fictitious addresses and locations throughout my shift to keep the criminals off balance. If I was out of town or even pulling into my driveway at the end of my shift, I would tell dispatch to "log a patrol check for the high school …" or wherever. I knew the crooks would hunker down and think I was in town. Who knows how many burglaries or crimes I prevented? Of course, I would tell my dispatch what I was doing. Sometimes, when I advised I was at a certain location, they would call my phone and ask, "Are you really there?" I love my dispatchers…

Whether you work in a busy metropolitan area or a rural substation alone, you will always have an opportunity to use unorthodox patrol procedures to solve the everyday problems we face in patrol. Being able to "think outside the box" gives you the advantage when hunting dopers and criminals. Finding unique ways to create activity and make arrests gives you a huge deal of personal satisfaction and helps you gain recognition with your peers and supervisors alike. Being creative doesn't mean you are "walking the line" and leaning toward corruption. Just because you don't follow the blind that make common sense mistakes everyday, doesn't mean you're being sneaky or crooked. Be creative and find new ways to solve crime and make arrests. Have fun with it and chances are your partners will start to follow you around. As I mentioned before, when you start to work street-level dope aggressively, you will naturally take on a leadership role and your partners who care and want to work will align themselves with you and together, you'll have a blast while making a difference in the community.

# EPILOGUE

Law enforcement is always changing and for us to be effective, we have to change too. From the time I started writing this book until now, I have changed. By now, I am certain you have likely changed too (or at least how you think about working dope) and now you probably know who I am and have realized that I am just like you. I have learned and struggled at times throughout my career and I have made more than my share of mistakes. As you read through this book you might have read something that sounded to you like a mistake. Well, that's okay. Case law evolves daily and those who have been in this job for any length of time have seen laws change and methods of operation change.

If one technique or trick has become obsolete from the time this book was written until the time you read it, it happens. The main points to take from this book and back with you to the streets are this. Drugs effect everything we do in law enforcement. Dope is at the core of nearly every call you will handle. To serve your community and do what you swore you would do, you must fight the cancer at the core. Make yourself an expert in everything drug related and use every common and unorthodox technique you can find to win. If you win as an individual police officer, you have done your part. Trust me, I will do my part.

Once you've finished reading this book, pass it along. Give it to your beat partner or the "rookie" and encourage them to read it. I never intended for this book to stand alone as "all encompassing" pertaining to street-level dope. If I did, I would still be writing because in this job you never stop learning. Share the information you have learned and pass it along. If you have a unique trick or technique that you have used in the field and it helped you make a case or arrest a bad guy, pass it along. My motivation for writing this book was to share information. I know when I was a new deputy trying to learn, finding how veteran cops worked dope, or any case for that matter, seemed impossible. Don't let that happen to your partners or your department. And, always be safe.